D1213234

Music at the Crossroads

Abram Chasins

Music at the Crossroads

THE MACMILLAN COMPANY,
NEW YORK, NEW YORK

COLLIER-MACMILLAN LIMITED, LONDON

ML
3795
.C43

Copyright © 1972 by Abram Chasins

All rights reserved. No part of this book may be reproduced or transmitted in any form or by any means, electronic or mechanical, including photo-copying, recording or by any information storage and retrieval system, without permission in writing from the Publisher.

The Macmillan Company
866 Third Avenue, New York, N.Y. 10022
Collier-Macmillan Canada Ltd., Toronto, Ontario

Library of Congress Catalog Card Number: 78-169232

First Printing

Printed in the United States of America

To Irl Allison, in appreciation of his
lifelong devotion and service to pianism

Acknowledgments

I am indebted to numerous artists, executives, managers, administrators, teachers, and students—those I have not named no less than those I have—who invited me to attend concerts and classes, and who generously provided outspoken answers to my often intrusive questions.

Deep appreciation is owed to my friend and colleague, Louis Chapin, who assumed the irksome job of taking many a messy batch of almost indecipherable notes and returning a coherent draft

ACKNOWLEDGMENTS

that I could mull over. Too often, as evolution moved with the speed of revolution, what I had notated was rendered obsolete in transit, which accounts for the six or seven rewrites that caused me to miss my contracted deadline, several times and by several years!

Perhaps this may suggest the infinite tolerance and understanding of my friend and editor, Joseph Elder. My warmest thanks to him for his Job-like patience and for his demonstration, through a long and tactful but firm series of do's and don't's, of devotion to the cause of English prose.

In addition, I owe thanks to Portia Merriam and to Stephen Joseph for reading galleys and making suggestions that I have followed gratefully.

Contents

Prelude

*E*ver since I began this book in 1967, it has been increasingly apparent that on every level of life and art we are on the brink of either heaven or hell—of a period of peace and revitalization or of violence and decay. The choice is no longer ours. My generation blew it sky high. Now it's up to the young people.

In the music world, classical and pop, everything has been turned upside down and inside out more than in any other half-decade in history. Actually, the latest phase of the musical revolution began early in the surging sixties. Already electronic sounds were erupting on every side; rock was no longer a fad but a compelling force whose protesting poetry and musical fluidity had captured the teenagers of the entire world; and the dizzy descent in the sales of classical recordings and concert tickets warned that the very future of musical culture was in jeopardy.

This book is an attempt to observe and to interpret the ferment—with all its conflicting tendencies—and to comment upon it for those to whom instrumental music and performance are matters of interest and concern. Inevitably, the range of my researches and inquiries is confined. My focal point is the hard realities of the field of instrumental music. This will not be taken, I trust, as lack of solicitude for composers or conductors or vocalists. On the contrary, the significance of their art and the magnitude of their problems demand separate studies.

However, any consideration of the status of instrumental music-making and the problems of the instrumentalist inevitably leads to matters pertinent not alone to all aspects of musical art but equally to music lovers and, more broadly, to life itself.

A Bird's-Eye View:
The Musical Scene "Like It Is"

Whether we are drummers or plumbers, bankers or physicians or farmers, this is our time and our world. War, inflation, education, ideological confrontation, civil and political strife— all the problems of our society are no more peculiar to the artist than to the non-artist. We are all in this maze together, and if we are to emerge at all, if we are to be as strong in ideas and ideals as in money and military might, the state and

1

fate of the arts must be an organic part of our national life.

Until recently, a book about music, even a non-technical one, was of interest to a limited, specialized audience. Nowadays, there is a vast public involved with all kinds of music or with some specific kind. Their interests lie far beyond mere sound: they have become deeply implicated in the products and personalities of music and greatly puzzled over their seething ramifications.

No less perplexed are the insiders, the professional musicians and those who merchandise their services, who add profound anxiety to the confusion. They are reaping what they finally recognize as the bitter fruits of the ecological disruption that the musical world itself has created. Those most affected by the upheaval are the youngsters who have been turned off by the paraphernalia of "serious music," and those most victimized are the ones who hope to make some sort of life in that rough-and-tumble field of human activity.

Of course, the musician's existence, even in former periods of patronage, was hardly ever tranquil. Yet for several centuries before the twentieth, the musical facts of life were at least considerate enough to stand reasonably still while observers tried to describe them. In our period, evolution moves not only at the dizzy pace of revolution, but also no less chaotically. Moreover, our cultural conditions are so entangled that no facet of art can any longer be isolated from another.

In our time and in our country, there were the fixed facts of white-tie-and-tails events—concerts, recitals, operas—all perpetuating a standard repertory with room at the edges only for carefully accredited new additions. Way over in left field were the "modern music" concerts, attended by devout disciples almost never to be found at any other sort of concert. This was the "classical" field.

Then, well across the tracks, there was "pop" music—anything from improvisational, free-swinging jazz to musical comedy—almost all of it ignored by the serious musicians and musical public.

Of course, things have never been quite *that* stable. Composers like Debussy, Ravel, Milhaud, Stravinsky, and Copland tried their hands at jazz idioms; and to Carnegie Hall came George Gershwin, Paul Whiteman, and Benny Goodman. All this was taken in good-humored, easy stride. After all, the musical world, like every other world, has long been in the throes of change, which, to be sure, is the unchanging face of history. And it was clear that these interminglings bore virtually no relation to the major issue of contemporary music, the frontal attack on tonality itself that was shaking the musical world to its roots.

3

Nevertheless, even this upheaval was mild compared with the ruthless discarding of all past ways of producing and projecting sounds, which we witnessed within the one decade of the sixties. Weekly, daily, even as we write these words, the revolution goes on. Description itself becomes reckless. Yet we must try to recognize and evaluate what is whirring and crashing by our heads, even as we duck. This no man's land—or is it suddenly everyman's land?—is, after all, where music is being composed, performed, and studied, where it is being heard and judged, accepted and rejected.

Briefly, what is happening has thrown every phase of music, traditional and modern, creative and interpretive, classical and popular, into a state of crisis. We are more likely to grasp this fact and its present meaning if we place it against the background of recent American musical life. In the fields of concert and opera, experimental schools have all but alienated the public with their dehumanized, artificial, and sterile products. About the only people who are listening to the most advanced composers, it seems, are the next most advanced. This is not to deny the composer's right to express his sense of the spiritual despair and emotional aridity of our age, but rather to defend the listener's corresponding right to accept what appeals to him and reject what does not.

4

Despite the abuses hurled at the musical lay-
man in those mythologies of music which for too
long have passed as histories, his record is one of
astute judgment. He had no trouble in selecting
the best composers and their best works, if not
immediately, then promptly. His choices, his favorites, remain the standard items of our concert and
opera repertories, from Bach through Stravinsky.
This same plain music lover has also been responsible for the fate of contemporary music. If he
found a work interesting enough to hear again,
it lived. If he came to love it, it became a popular
classic in its own time, according to an age-old
incontestable process still going on right now.

Well and good. But the proven masterpieces of
any age are only a tiny percentage of the total it
produced, and the few works that have sifted
through the past three centuries have now been
played over and over again to a satiated and diminishing public. Not even a prestigious personality
or an exciting ensemble or production can be
counted on to pack halls and guarantee high prices
for the umpteenth "interpretation" of an all-Bee-
thoven recital or Tchaikovsky's *Pathétique* or Ver-
di's *Aida*.

To be sure, there's always a new generation
coming up, and some of its members will undoubtedly discover new classics as their parents and

5

grandparents did. But the trouble now is that the audience is not growing even remotely in pace with the population.

As for "modern music" in the classical field, the occasional big-city concerts of the avant garde have moved further and further away from the mainstream of the concert auditoriums into the colleges and universities, where, to quote Stravinsky, "sheltered composers compose and perform for each other in secret languages."

Does this mean that esoteric concerts are unproductive, so much wasted effort and money? Not necessarily. It is under academic auspices, after all, that some of the most promising lines of experimentation have been initiated, developed, and subsidized.

Academic institutions have provided ideal conditions for the electronic transformation of sound, which appeared in the late forties. In this technique, which at first used either musical tones or indeterminate noises as raw material, everything is recorded on tape and then subjected to a complete metamorphosis—speeded up, slowed down, played backwards, treated to an unlimited variety of distortions of pitch, timbre, duration, and dynamics. The chief transmitters of instruments in this new world of superhuman vibration are the playback machine and the loudspeaker.

Another branch of electronic music has emerged in which the sound itself is generated not from natural but from purely electronic sources. This emancipated the style still more completely from precedent.

"Random" or aleatory music may or may not be electronic. In either case its score is a diagram which allows certain choices to each of several players. John Cage, the American hero of the happening, has exploited it in electronic terms, and various other musicians have devised pieces in which a notated musical idea is dealt with by the players according to a flexible scheme that evolves entirely from their decisions of the moment.

Interesting as these works are in theory, their performances have been given before ever smaller and specialized, ever more bewildered, bothered, and unbewitched audiences, even while the patronage of completely unproblematical contemporary compositions has been dwindling.

Where, then, are the big crowds and the white-hot enthusiasms? Where are the excited music lovers who seek out and support the latest compositions, performers, and recordings? Where, in short, is the "action"? Where the young people are, those who are passionately involved, who are staging various revolutions according to their own sphere of opinion. Their reaction is leveled against sterile modernism, against the tired routines of the Establishment, and especially against the European-minded elite's put-down of our native musical resources, our pop music, our folk music.

Jazz, derived from African sources and developed in our country in the first half of this century, has a history as dramatic as it is revealing. Originated by musically illiterate, segregated blacks, this potent, syncopated, and infectious music emerged as an unwritten, improvised phenomenon without status. To an incredible extent, discrediting the entire world of so-called serious music, this most idiomatic of American idioms has remained, as have all other black cultural achievements, insufficiently appreciated by whites except for a small number of great and grateful jazz musicians.

"Actually," writes Henry Pleasants in his fine book, *Serious Music and All That Jazz,* "since its origins were plebeian, and Negro plebeian at that, and since the white community first became aware of it as music for dancing, every assessment of it was governed by habits of evaluation in a social context. Not even its practitioners or those who were captured by its primitive vigor, thought of jazz as anything but irretrievably lowbrow."

So it was that pop music was the victim of the snobbery and racism of our European-oriented musical community, which has never ceased proclaim-

8

ing its tolerance and broad-mindedness, its un-
prejudiced receptivity to new ideas. Nothing has
been more costly to our musical development than
this segregation of jazz, except, perhaps, the slav-
ish dependence of our musical Establishment upon
European systems and isms, which led it into a
creative impasse.

Meanwhile, the pop movement flourished,
whether it was called ragtime, swing, bop, rhythm-
and-blues, country-and-western, gospel, rock, or
soul. I assume that none of us wants to become
embroiled in tiresome arguments over what is and
what isn't *real* jazz. My point is that while the
creators and the players of jazz were building an
art that was accepted and loved the world over, except by a disdainful Establishment that knows
nothing about it, the "classical" avant garde was
erecting an ever higher wall between itself and the
concert public.

The reaction was inevitable. Young people, especially, rebelled with unprecedented force against
the composers who, contemptuous of "popularity,"
tried to outdo each other in incomprehensibility.
In the past, youngsters were ready to be led,
through their university and community concert
series, to drink at the fount of high art. These
days, though, classical performers are beginning to
cast inquiring glances elsewhere.

Where are they looking? Where are they going? Which, if any, of the many current tendencies and techniques will become the musical style of the future? What combination of qualities and skills will be demanded of the next generation of ambitious young musicians? What new culture will evolve and what will it require from the listener?

The answers to these questions are being sought everywhere by everyone—composers, performers, managers, educators, students, and the musical public alike. Of one thing we can be certain: there are no simple answers that will solve our pluralistic problems. But meet them we must and head on.

I have a hunch it will pay off, handsomely.

2

The Urge to Merge

*T*he short shrift that "serious" music has handed "popular" music from the beginning shows that it has yet to learn the fundamental lesson in classification that a delightful Brahms story could have taught.

At a Viennese ball a lady handed her fan to the famous composer to autograph. Examining it, Brahms noticed that the fan was inscribed with the first two measures of *The Blue Danube Waltz* by Johann Strauss. Turning it over, Brahms signed it with the words: "Unfortunately not by Johannes Brahms."

The American musical Establishment had to see its audiences vanishing and the audiences for jazz and rock festivals mount astronomically before it deigned to lend an ear to our most indigenous music.

But popular music had its own insularities. By the early fifties, the whining, self-pitying lyrics of unrequited love, the June-moon rhyming, and the slick, sugary song-and-dance tunes of musical comedy were turning the public stomach. For a while, as the prevailing product became more and more artificial, the entire industry suffered heavily. Then, and then only, Tin Pan Alley got a whiff of some bracing air blowing from a different direction, which drew its habitués out of their Broadway cubicles into a more nourishing atmosphere.

The revolution to which pop music turned a deaf ear had been gathering for some time. For decades, in spite of the work of pioneers like Alan and John Lomax and Carl Sandburg, the rich crop of American folk music lay unharvested. Then, as singers like Richard Dyer Bennet and John Jacob Niles used it for recital purposes, there began to emerge a strong, folk-oriented music generally classified as country-and-western. Its songs descended from the Scotch, Irish, and English settlers, among the earliest white inhabitants of North America. The music of these people had a simple charm and moving depth, its lyrics a straightforward sincerity of language. Above all, the ballads were as unmistakably genuine as the twangy dialects that characterized them.

Tin Pan Alley's first attempts to learn the trick that made country music tick were unsuccessful. It could never quite capture the spirit of the gospel-loving mountaineers or the rough-riding cattlemen of the range, and settled instead for adaptations of the New Orleans and Chicago jazz that could be easily exploited commercially in sheet music and recording sales.

Country music, however, persisted on its own and swept the world. In Germany, for example, native bands began to abandon even Johann Strauss's waltzes in favor of the high-pitched hoedown music of Arkansas and Kentucky. They recognized country music as a truly native American expression. On Saturday night it could mean singing and dancing to the accompaniment of a fiddle and a guitar—music-making stripped of all pretensions—and on Sunday morning it could embrace hymns and songs that echoed the deepest human feelings and spiritual longings.

Early in the fifties, Bill Haley, an athletic country singer from the Midwest, made a record called

13

"Rock Around the Clock." It was the theme music of the film *The Blackboard Jungle* and became an international smash, which was soon followed by a couple of records by a white country boy from Mississippi whose voice and style were characteristically black. Featuring a wild-swinging guitar technique and surrounded by a driving accompaniment, Elvis Presley's first disks to cross the Mason-Dixon line brought an instantaneous explosion. Not even the virtual unintelligibility of the words could keep every one of his recordings from becoming a world-wide hit and soaring over the million mark in sales.

Clearly a major shift was overdue. A fusion of country-and-western, rhythm-and-blues, of black and white music, was the first big step. The late Cleveland disk jockey Alan Freed named it "rock 'n' roll," a phrase taken from an old jazz blues. Many other singers and banjoists and guitarists contributed their bit to the early evolution; and then out of an unlikely Liverpool came the Beatles, just in time to save rock from becoming as self-conscious and mannered as jazz.

This remarkable quartet not only rescued but redeemed rock 'n' roll. Putting their ears to the groundswell of folk style, they revitalized rock with poetic and significant lyrics, with their imaginative tunes and inventive harmonizations, with an inti-

14

mate attitude toward their music-making and their audiences. Through them, rock became a cultural force to reckon with, a vehement force that expressed the deepest emotions and motivations of youth throughout the world.

Rock 'n' roll alone expresses the youth community's feelings about society, war, economics, human relationships, everything that is life. Rock has created a style that makes it the inevitable artistic way to register protest, a style that has shaped the desire for liberation on every front, a style that voices freedom from crippling repressions.

Not only adolescents have been rocked. In Paris, I met the seventy-five-year-old Darius Milhaud, who greeted me excitedly, saying, "I read your article on the Beatles just before I left the States, and the first thing I did when I arrived here was to hear their records. They are fantastic! And their taste and sound and diction! I agree with you: they are really extraordinary.

"But how much they will influence the future music, I would not dare to predict. Music and life are very much alike. I'll never forget how after World War I everyone was certain there would never be another war—only serenity and peace and joy. What idiots we were! And of course you know that I was a member of the famous—maybe I should say infamous—*Les Six*, the avant garde of the avant garde, and what idiots *we* were! In ten years, we were the *rear garde*. In twenty years, we were dead or you would have thought so. *Mon Dieu*, do you realize that Pierre Boulez already belongs to the *last* generation! Who can make predictions? But I know something is happening, and it could attract the biggest musical public in history. And there I go, predicting again!"

Meanwhile, back on New York's 57th Street, the concert managers were beginning to get the signal (not that their getting it has yet added up to a thing). It was as clear as red ink that young audiences were forsaking concert halls unless the heroes and heroines of pop were appearing there, and were flocking downtown to such havens as the Electric Circus and Fillmore East. There they could reverberate not only to a deafening rock group but also, in a simultaneous splash, to such prestigious and subtle antiquarians as the New York Pro Musica. That old pro Sol Hurok proclaimed that "a big change has been taking place. We must not ignore the youth of this country today. We have to get them to concerts and somehow to cater to them."

The obvious comment (as universities repair their windows and replace their presidents, as 300,000 youngsters congregate on a Catskill hillside for an August weekend of rock and love and marijuana) would seem to be: "Just try to ignore the youth of this country today!"

Quite naturally, as classical music bumbled into a cul-de-sac, and jazz hit its own dead end, rock became the living musical art. Everything within reach has been thrown into its weird brew: the whole gamut of atonalism, jazz, Indian raga, Baroque, electronic—you name it, it is to be found somewhere in this exciting, infinitely aleatory, ecstatic potpourri, this psykaleidoscope of collision. Everything, that is, except what adults called romanticism, and some form of what may yet turn out to be a synthesizing ingredient. Actually, the counter-revolution has been under way for some time now in the sweet 'n' low idiom of the new rock.

Near the heart of this multifarious merger is a meeting between the techniques of rock and jazz, whose exponents wouldn't at one time come within a discotheque of each other.

"The change has come about," wrote John S. Wilson in the *New York Times*, "because musicians of both schools have found themselves working toward what they feel is a dead end and, in their dissatisfaction, each school has been attracted by the seemingly new horizons of the other school."

He tells of Steve Marcus, a jazz saxophonist who has been featured in Woody Herman's and Stan

17

Kenton's bands, going through a period of surrep-
titiously enjoying the Beatles' records, after which
he formed a small group which he described as "a
jazz band that uses the colors of rock." But Don
Sebeskey, an experienced trombonist-arranger, told
Wilson that "the new musicians are listening to
jazz, looking for more complex patterns. As they
grow as musicians, they will demand more complex
music to play." More mature than complex, one
hopes, for conscious contrivance was the very trap
into which the neo-classicists and atonalists fell.

It speaks well for rock that so literate and honest
a musical team as Paul Simon and Arthur Garfunkel, whose lyrics show a hunger for meaning and
an ear for poetry, could make their way to the big
time; that it can accommodate not only the non-
virtuosic Beatles but also the Juilliard-bred New
York Rock and Roll Ensemble, as adept at Handel
and Couperin as they are at their own rock speci-
mens; that Bach can come a little further into his
own through the "switched on" reverberations of a
Moog synthesizer or through the extraordinary
vocalizing of his instrumental music by the Swingle
Singers from France. And for that matter, both
credit and profit have accrued to such old-line
sanctuaries as Carnegie Hall, the Tanglewood Shed,
and the Brooklyn Academy of Music, for joining

18

THE URGE TO MERGE

the Electric Circus and Fillmore East in playing
host to such hybrid experiences.

It should be admitted, however, that the younger
generation isn't always turned on by the electronic
switch. It has to work right. At one of Leonard
Bernstein's Young People's Concerts with the New
York Philharmonic, the audience warmed more to
a straight performance of Bach's *Fifth Brandenburg
Concerto*, the first movement, than they did to a
souped-up version for Moog synthesizer of the
Little Organ Fugue in G Minor, distorted by faulty
amplifying equipment. Concluding the program, by
the way, was a set of rock variations and a fantasy
on the *Brandenburg* movement by the New York
Rock and Roll Ensemble. To me, it was great fun
and provocative. The kids went wild and laughed
their heads off in delight.

Do we have any mixed-media masterpieces yet?
Good Lord, no! Perhaps it's enough for now that
the producers are getting away from the appalling
sterility and paralyzing sameness of classical avant
gardism and from the clichés and mannerisms of
effete popular music. In doing so, of course, they
sometimes labor to concoct an *atmosphere* of
masterpiece-in-the-making. Not long ago, for example, the Electric Circus staged a mixed-media
electronic happening by John Cage called *Reunion*,

complete with color projections; the several sounds of blenders mixing drinks and of Gordon Mumma reading an essay through a synthesizer; a corps of dial-twisting technicians; and at the center of it all Cage himself, playing chess in impassive silence on a board that was wired so as to affect the noise everywhere else. With all due respect to a tireless innovator, and much less of same to his submissive audience, this kind of ritual would seem to be 99 and 44/100 per cent humbug.

What, then, does the new, rock-oriented burst of creativity have going for it, which under less self-conscious leadership *may* yet produce a masterpiece? It has, of course, the immeasurable energy and spontaneity and self-confidence of youth. But it has roots, too—stronger American roots than the disembodied, Europe-oriented avant garde.

The critic Eric Salzman (who, incidentally, helped to initiate the Electric Circus) pointed this out in 1965 in an article on the new music that he contributed to Richard Kostelanetz's *The New American Arts:* "The avant garde is an essentially European phenomenon, irrelevant to ... the American tradition of handwork, of doing things, of tinkering, of activity as a good and an end in itself; it is alien to the American experience of the frontier, of the idea of the extension of possibility, of conformity on the one hand and freedom of action on the other, of mass-cult—ugly, brutal, closed on one side—and multiplicity—always open at some other, almost unknown, outer end.

"Thus . . . we can begin to define the preconditions of the new American music in terms of pluralism and the extension of the idea of the possible."

In the context of such a comment, the most characteristically American classical composers come to mind: the heel-kicking restlessness of Louis Moreau Gottschalk; the wide-open, baling-wire experimentalism of Charles Ives, who rocked his corner of Connecticut in the late nineties by creating the effect of two bands approaching a placid village green from opposite directions, playing the same march in sharply different keys; the intense, craggy chromaticism of Carl Ruggles; the many ingenuities of Henry Cowell; the space-pioneering of Edgard Varèse; not to mention that doughty colonial tanner William Billings, some of whose jogging anthems were charged with political protest.

Who can say, then, whether this inborn American flair for "the extension of possibility" may not be breaking out as popular art with a vehemence that Salzman himself could not have predicted in 1965, though he described its makings?

One bracing feature of this musical amalgamation is the increasing prominence of improvisation with both Baroque and jazz styles. This means that the performer has again arisen as the partner of the composer—and not only in those places where the composer allocates to the performer most of the responsibility for working out detail or even structural design. Today, the small combos that dominate the performance field encourage the utmost flexibility in interpretation and ornamentation, inviting all kinds of experiments, and drawing ideas from every region of music.

The destination of these crosscurrents remains the big question, but the amalgamation is full of life for music right now.

And how, finally, does it bear on careers in music? Perhaps, at the moment, more in regard to the whole study of music and to the musician's attitude than anything else. Though specialized skills and a clear sense of identity will always be valuable assets, where the urge to merge is given free rein, no man (to paraphrase John Donne) can be a stylistic island. Not even, perhaps, John Cage's kind of avant garde island. Or the island represented, say, by the third desk of the second violins in a big symphony orchestra, whose tonal mass might seem to be insulation enough for anyone. John Lewis, a musician who tried with his Orchestra U.S.A. to show symphony orchestras what they had been missing in the interpretation of jazz, has more recently been taking his Modern Jazz Quartet to play as soloists with a long list of symphonies from Montreal to San Diego, arousing packed halls to hysteria.

A Sunday *New York Times* piece reports the alert Lewis's opinion that every symphony orchestra should have a resident composer experienced in jazz, for at least a year, to show how to communicate its unique rhythms and moods.

"Jazz has grown up enough so that its characteristics are sufficiently sophisticated for concert works. When we play with an orchestra, the concerts are sold out. . . . We played three concerts in Corpus Christi and filled a two-thousand-seat hall each time." A pension-fund concert at twice the price brought ten thousand!

A few prestigious composers have unbent enough to cast a paternal glance at elements of jazz, though they have behaved like society snobs in mansions living next door to beggars in hovels. That's the way such elegant householders as Debussy, Ravel, Stravinsky, and Copland leaned over the fence to borrow a cup of melodic sugar, a saucer of blues, a pinch of rhythm ad lib. Each one appears to have been left with a rather bitter aftertaste, suggesting that these ingredients do not blend. Perhaps they are basically incompatible, but all it will take is the right genius to make such a statement absurd.

Meanwhile, during the past several decades, the neighborliness has grown on both sides as the jazz folk, from Gershwin to Brubeck, began running across the lawn to borrow somewhat weightier items such as orchestration, harmonization, larger structures, and now the whole apparatus of electronicism.

Definitely, a change of heart and mind is gradually coming about. There are at least a dozen universities and a half-dozen music conservatories (by publication time, there will be many more, I am certain) that offer instruction and degree-credit courses in jazz. At the last conference of music educators in Seattle, an invitation to the National Association of Jazz Educators was issued, accepted and, one assumes, fruitfully utilized, for within a year the long overdue revival of jazz, which had been cruelly rocked by rock, was an accomplished fact. And fervently one hopes that the greatest jazz musicians are still around in sufficient health and spirit to demonstrate America's finest indigenous music and to teach our youth an art that the rock rage made less accessible.

The fortunate young people who have been exposed to the classical and jazz mainstreams as well as to rock, and even to Gunther Schuller's "third stream" (his own hybrid of symphonic techniques and the pulse of jazz) have no stylistic prejudice at all. They have no hesitation or inhibition about playing a Jelly Roll Morton record immediately before, or a Blood, Sweat and Tears album immediately after, a Vivaldi concerto.

I recently heard the seventy-fifth anniversary concert of the Third Street Music School Settlement, one of those turn-of-the-century establishments designed to get children off the streets of a ghetto neighborhood. At first, music was mainly a convenient excuse to keep kids from fighting and stealing. Its function was social and rehabilitory. Now, as the school's director Harris Danziger explained in a newspaper interview following the concert, "We occupy a space between the public school system and the preparatory departments of the big conservatories." For some time this venerable institution has built music closely into the daily life of our young people, and in doing so also has trained a large number of professionals.

And what sort of program marked the gala celebration? At one moment we were regaled by a sixteenth-century madrigal of Orlando di Lasso and in the next, without pause, by a twentieth-century rock number from the musical *Hair*. If this proximity was meant as a quick twist of the shower handle, even for those of us who felt it, the cold douse was exceedingly amusing and bracing. For the kids, the question of "contrast" or incompatibility never existed. They are too interested in music as music, too busy conquering their own musical world. They couldn't care less about the controversies raging under their feet and above their heads. Literary criticism and esthetic debate are so much mint sauce to them; they're after the meat of the matter.

Music "sends" these kids and at a very early age. Many of them who haven't the foggiest desire of becoming professional musicians are more sophisticated than many serious-minded, career-bent students who attend conservatories or colleges that cling to outworn and inadequate methods. Again Danziger: "We teach theory with guitar as well as with piano. I'm amazed to hear these youngsters in just a couple of weeks of training, calling out terribly involved chords: 'That's a D-flat major 13th with a passing note in the soprano,' they say, evidently hearing chords as entities." One tot showed me his assigned homework: learning to beat out rhythms whose complexities and notation struck the same terror in my heart that I experienced when my nephew showed me the "new math."

Such training is not merely altruistic busy work, but practical job preparation. The music school's alumni include many eminent musicians, composers, soloists, musicologists, and at this moment six graduates who play in the New York Philharmonic and several who sit in the Metropolitan Opera Orchestra. "And they'll be able to handle whatever is thrown at them," said Danziger. "The electronic synthesizer, for example. It's a teaching tool that we consider a musical counterpart to clay in art classes. We start right out to show the tots four to six years old that music is something they not only perform but will also have to create."

That statement is very much what this chapter is all about. Not only in the foreseeable future but right this minute, the conservatories, colleges, and universities, which are not preparing their students to understand and handle all the newer trends, are turning out a lot of unemployables. That, one regrets to say, is what all but perhaps two dozen institutions throughout the entire United States are doing to some extent if not completely.

Among the strongest exceptions are three schools widely separated geographically and chronologically —the venerable Music Education Division of New York University, the Berklee College of Music in Boston, and the recently endowed California Institute of the Arts, the latter under construction in a suburb of Los Angeles while its concepts and curriculum, its classes and faculty and lecturers are being fully formulated. Mel Powell has left his post as chairman of the composition faculty of Yale to become dean of the music school, and he has already formed a faculty that includes Nicholas England, ethnomusicologist and African specialist; Morton Subotnick, electronic specialist in multimedia techniques; the Ghanaian drummers, Alfred and Seth Ladzekpo; James Tenny, computer specialist; Leonard Stein, noted theoretician; Ravi Shankar, and still others. But one gets the idea, especially with the further information that interaction among all the schools of the institute will be fundamental, that there will be no fixed curriculum as such and no grades. Fluidity, mastery, versatility are the prime objectives.

For over twenty-five years, the Berklee College has succeeded singularly by determining the technical needs of music students and by acquiring a faculty with the skills to supply them. On these simple premises and practices, it has produced an alumni whose creative and interpretive achievements adorn an impressive list of imaginative concert works, recordings, films, and stage works. Yet, not one "serious musician" to whom I mentioned it had ever heard of it, which most possibly is explainable on the gloomy grounds that for most of its life, popular musicians have called it "The Jazz School."

According to its founder and president, Lawrence Berk, this coeducational and independent music college has over 1,500 students, more than 100 of them from thirty-five foreign countries, "attributable to a basic educational philosophy of relevance and involvement."

Vice-president Lee Berk says, "The Berklee objective is to provide an integrated curriculum for the development of the professionally competent musician who, upon graduation, is qualified to successfully meet any musical challenge in his chosen career as music educator, instrumentalist, composer or arranger."

How is this task accomplished at Berklee? By the most thorough theoretical training immediately utilized and developed through practical creation and performance while he learns. At all stages of acquiring techniques, at all levels of musicianship, self-expression is stimulated through group demonstration and performance. Improvisational programs, modular and electronic techniques, even legal protection of musical property are among an impressively practical yet vital curriculum that features over three hundred ensemble groups in rehearsal each week. In the film scoring department, students actually create sound tracks, edit film, learn to use all equipment pertinent to sound films. Even English courses demand record and concert reviews, critical essays and comments on all kinds of compositions and performances.

"At my alma mater," said Quincy Jones ('52)

who on that very day in 1970 received his fifth
Grammy Award nomination, "every minute is an
exciting experience: you're either learning something or trying it out; you're either hearing something or creating or performing something yourself.
I'll tell you, man, you're either 'turned on' all the
time or you're soon turned out. That's Berklee and
it's great!"

Local institutions, please copy.

New York University announces new courses in
Afro-American music, contemporary American music, including rock, jazz, multimedia concepts (and
all other idioms that claim attention), and an expanded course in music therapy. The division's development is being guided by Jerrold Ross. Still in
his mid-thirties, he has always been an articulate
spokesman for the "complete musician," which he
himself exemplifies: one who seeks to communicate
on all levels.

Ross is no anarchist. He uses and invokes the
complete resources of the university whenever they
promise results. In the music therapy courses, for
example, he calls upon the cooperation of the medical division. His first goal is "to teach artists to
reach the minds and hearts of all."

The last time I heard that kind of talk was at
Madison Square Garden in New York where sixteen thousand people, mainly youngsters, stood for

hours to hear the Rolling Stones in the last of
three consecutive concerts at that mammoth hall,
sold out night after night. I asked a seventeen-year-
old boy why he had come every night, and if he
had had to make any personal sacrifices to pay the
ticket charge of eight dollars a performance. "When
they sing and play, I get goose bumps because
they're doing it for *me*. And they give me everything they have. They hold nothing back, not a
thing. That's why I'm here and keep coming. The
money? Oh, I operate a computer after school, every
day for three hours, five days a week. I get a hundred bucks. If I didn't, I'd go standing for two
bucks. Man, you don't talk about money when
someone makes you happy, takes you outa this
lousy world for a while."

I wished someone had told me something like
that when I was performing. I wished that every
composer and performer whose abdication of the
responsibility to communicate has accelerated, if
not motivated, the current crisis in our musical culture, had been exposed to this no-nonsense attitude
of holding artists and their art to strict personal
account.

"I see what you mean," I said.

"Glad you see it my way," he added, "'cause
that's the blunt cool, man."

3

Talents and Yachts

*N*ever could I stretch my conscience to the point of calling a book or even a chapter "How to Become a Successful Instrumentalist." But in these days it seems reasonable to assume that quite a few readers may come to this book seeking specific information about musical professions. As we know, music is now so meaningful an experience to so many people, and its happenings and personalities hold so much fascination for the general reader that even its backstage problems are matters of normal public interest.

Throughout my professional life, many young people, mostly pianists, but also violinists, cellists, clarinetists, and others, have asked me to hear them play. Invariably, they ask if they "have what it takes" to make solo concert careers, to which I always say, "Certainly not!" And always they protest hotly, demanding to know, "How can you say such a thing even before hearing me play one note?"

My explanation would be something like J. P. Morgan's celebrated reply to a neophyte tycoon who once inquired about the cost of running a yacht. "You can't afford it," Morgan is reputed to have answered. "If you have to *ask* the upkeep, you can't afford one."

Translated into musical terms, anyone who thinks there is any choice in this matter of a solo career, has already revealed that the "call" isn't strong enough to endure what it takes. Music is a calling rather than a profession.

To illustrate, all we have to do is to observe those who are fully and fortunately launched, the successful soloists. Although they can perform pretty much where and when and at what fee they designate, even they cannot avoid the necessary hardships and responsibilities.

Here is a partial list of "musts" to be endured by one and all: long hours of backbreaking practice; on tour, the "cuisine" that often compels a choice between ptomaine and malnutrition, and no liquor for solace; performing not when or where the mood strikes, but at the given place and given moment dictated by contract; sleeping in a different bed each night or sometimes doing without one when crisis compels a night ride on a bus or plane; traveling in trains that should have saddles instead of seats; perpetual struggles against intrusions on privacy. All these rigors, and many I have resisted mentioning, require the digestion of a peasant, the resignation of a Trappist monk, and the constitution of a heavyweight champion.

And that's the life, the hard, lonely life of one who "has it made." Those who waver, who *think* they might try, who ask questions, had better quit *subito*. The only thing I've ever learned about talent, real talent, is that it includes a compulsion to do your own thing or "bust." Shall I, shall I not? are questions unrelated to the compelling inner force that must be obeyed, even if obedience means every sacrifice, starvation included. If you have this sort of drive, you won't be deterred by anything. If you don't, the chances are that you will not succeed. Rarely have I met a successful man who has not stressed how much of his success he owes to ignoring the advice he received.

At this moment, however, observing a world that offers entirely new conditions, including the possibility that today's fact may become tomorrow's falsehood, one can be more encouraging to talented young musicians with realistic goals and with equal talent for work and for learning. In music, to be forewarned is not to be forearmed, not by a long shot. But the facts of musical performance are not without a certain grim charm, even though knowing them carries limited advantage.

Each solo career is unique, each artist is a law unto himself, and that is his strength, his magnetism, his bag. He plays for the highest stakes, but as we know, there is no use pointing out the awful odds against him. His disdain for that is also part of his charisma. The world loves a winner against odds, and the winner takes all—including the responsibilities and the raps. In this, music is like any other game. Our national need in sport or art or entertainment is still for heroes to worship rather than for achievement to respect. We are demonstrably able to produce splendidly equipped artists as well as sportsmen, and for many years we have been consistently producing the best all-round musicians to be found anywhere. Few are geniuses, but there's no reason why we should expect that they be. When has genius been anything but rare?

Yet, few care that, unlike virtually any other endeavor, there is so little correspondence between a musician's ability and his reputation, between what he can do and what he can sell it for. In our society it is little cause for concern when a musician who has won the toughest contests against the world's best competitors or has garnered praise and plaudits from several continents is still unknown and waiting. Waiting for what? Waiting for some dramatic gimmick (murdering his manager, for example?) to connect a precious supply with a latent demand.

Throughout history, most artists have been reconciled to the lower rungs of the economic ladder. If we had valued the practitioners of law and medicine as we have those of music, there would be virtually no lawyers or doctors. But now, musicians are growing as worldly as other professionals, as concerned about the graphs and charts of the concert and recording business as the music merchants are with profit and loss. This is a realistic, healthy development, for the performing arts and artists are undergoing a financial crisis, just as the creative and educational fields are in an esthetic crisis. Unless the musical world realizes the seriousness of its present condition, it can only grow progressively worse.

36

Nowadays, I listen carefully and hopefully for a question other than, "Do I have what it takes to make a solo career?" If, for example, someone asks, "Is there a fair chance of making some sort of a life and a living in music today?"—that's something else again. And so is a statement I heard from a talented young pianist: "Music means everything to me. I'll do *anything* to be in music—anything, that is, short of having my family do without just so I can indulge myself. If I work like hell, what do you think my chances are?"

I think they are just fine and I said so, adding, "for anyone who says he'll do *anything*, and means *anything*. First, make sure that you have a really fine teacher, who will help you to equip yourself so thoroughly that you will be able to bring distinction to whatever opportunities arise. There is always room at the top, and the field is tremendous. Shoot for the soloist moon if you must, but be so versatile and so flexible that you could conduct, arrange, accompany, play chamber music, or teach, or even manage an orchestra capably. And if your chosen field of music does not offer anything immediately, be ready to assume whatever else may present itself in any of the many allied branches of music such as radio, films, recordings, publishing, etc. With this kind of preparation, and it will take working 'like hell,' you won't have to have too much luck

MUSIC AT THE CROSSROADS

to be a happy and a successful man, I promise you."

This I said with utmost conviction, despite the fact that pianists have the hardest time as soloists because they play the most widely studied of all musical instruments. Although the violinist, cellist, and clarinetist, to mention the other most common solo instrumentalists, face virtually the identical problems as the pianist who hopes for a virtuoso career, they have a tremendous economic advantage over the pianist, because there are so many orchestral opportunities for first-class musicians who do not insist upon playing only solo recitals and concertos with orchestras.

One of my happiest experiences concerns a cherubic oboist of seventeen, a highly gifted boy with a wide range of tastes and interests. He was studying with a first-desk player of a major orchestra who also "doubles" on bassoon for recording sessions and for commercial TV shows. This gentleman also teaches, when an unusually talented and ambitious youngster comes along, such as the one I was auditioning. "Why did you come to me?" I asked. "I'd like your opinion on what instrument I might 'double' on," he said. "The bassoon is not for me." I then asked him who, outside of his teacher, was his "favorite musician." Without waiting a second, he said, "Oh, Solly Goodman, over at the Philharmonic. Gee—that's what I call rhythm, man." I said, "Well, why don't you emulate your idol? Take up drums." That was five years ago. The last two years, that young man has turned down twice the number of jobs he accepts. He is enviously adjustable and adjusted. At his regular post with a major symphony, he revels in the music of Beethoven, Ravel, and Stravinsky, and then gets another kind of "bang" whamming at his drums at pop recording sessions. This boy really has it made. He loves his work and his life. Last year he earned over forty thousand dollars, this year around sixty, and all this at an age when most young men cannot even decide what they want to do. Of course, from such a case of exceptional qualities perfectly fulfilled, one can't draw many generalizations, but the solidity and versatility of such training are worth noting.

Any musician with the tangible assets of talent, intelligence, and industry should have no hesitancy in choosing a non-soloist career today, regardless of the uncertainties that plague music. My basis for optimism, however tentative, is not meager, for its main premise is that there will always be sufficient musical activity to sustain a need for outstanding instrumentalists in a cruelly competitive field so overcrowded with mediocrities.

Other encouraging signs are ever-increasing federal, state, and municipal subsidies, foundation interest, and awareness by business that its participation in the artistic activity of a community (still pathetically puny) has a direct bearing on corporate image. Musicians also find themselves members of powerful unions that have finally acquired control of the very viability of organizations that require their services. There is growing managerial concern in the individual artist and in the new world he faces. And finally the most promising factor is the possibility of some unifying catalyst arising to attract the huge numbers of pop-mad young music lovers to *all* music or music-making. So it was in the dear days of yore, musical mythology notwithstanding, when great art was great entertainment and proud of it. Meanwhile, whatever hold classical music still has on the hard core of ticket buyers and record buffs is due to our orchestral supremacy and to a few magnetic soloists, though the ever-mounting economic pressures are causing even them to hold on with clenched fists.

Doing extremely well are a relatively small number of solo artists near the top, who are busily playing, making fairly good money, and skinning their knuckles knocking wood. All others who have aspired to stardom have learned the hard way that the chances of a soloist being catapulted even to a near-top spot have diminished drastically.

Were it possible to discover the elements that

make for artistry and stardom, it would not prove very helpful, for their combination in right proportion would be as induplicable as the human being who possesses them. An inexplicable quality has always accounted for the public idol. Updated as "charisma," its composition still defies analysis and baffles us no less than it did generations of Broadway playwrights and producers, Hollywood moguls, opera impressarios, *and* concert managers.

With very few exceptions, neither the formerly traditional New York recital or orchestral debut with the untraditional rave reviews, nor success in a major international competition, nor even prestigious management command the leverage they once did. In our day, making it big is the exception— and in a surprising number of cases none of the above classic factors plays a part.

Artur Rubinstein once said, "Success is a game of roulette. Take it from a man who has played it a lot. One day a city or a nation doesn't know you're alive. The next day, they're killing themselves to get near you." Rubinstein knows, for this is exactly what happened to him, but not "the next day." Not until he was in his fifties did this former child prodigy's number come up. Paderewski's first tours were flops, everywhere. Van Cliburn's gifts and personality were exposed to thousands, but his

41

career had just about ground to a halt until his victory in the Soviet Union's Tchaikovsky contest launched him into orbit.

What governs these things? Talent? Personal glamour, brilliantly exploited by a dynamic publicity machine? Being at the right spot at the right moment? We've seen any and all of these elements flattened by the utterly unaccountable glacier of public apathy.

Lucky are those who have not had to endure the frustration of mass indifference. Also lucky are those who have, but have remained psychologically sound, for with soloist or near-soloist equipment, a well-balanced musician has strong prospects for a satisfying and remunerative career, especially if he plays an orchestral instrument. This is true despite the fact that several hundred symphonic organizations, including those at the top, are groveling for adequate support.

Everyone knows about the serious shortage of good string players, but anyone who wants to know the actual need for good instrumentalists generally should take a look at the publications of the American Federation of Musicians. If this is of little interest to you, pass on the suggestion to some sister or brother whose interest it may serve, for those publications carry truly handsome offers for an amazing number of jobs in all sections of quality orchestras. Most of them are in the major orchestras of cities outside of New York where, I was about to write, "musicians are a drug on the market." O tempora! O mores! Pardon the digression. Now, back to musical jobs.

The situation boils down to this: an adequately equipped musician, who does not insist upon a soloist career, and who does not insist upon working in the most overcrowded and oversupplied cities, will have a wide choice of splendid posts available to him. The sort of positions and the location I refer to can be combined with related activities like teaching, lecturing, recording, and playing chamber music and/or dance music for a fascinating, remunerative, and bustling life in "doing what comes naturally." Minimum salaries: fifteen thousand dollars annually, and upwards. Later these possibilities will be scrutinized more closely.

Why, then, are so many, including the Department of Labor, so discouraging? To answer adequately, one is bound to dig under the speculative quicksand of "making it big" down to the bedrock of minimal requirements for a musician and performer—whether he ends up performing on sold-out international tours or before occasional audiences of admiring friends and neighbors at the local lodge hall.

The requirements include first of all the achieving of certain standards in technical ability and interpretation, based on serious study, long and consistent hours of practice, absolute dedication, and unflagging discipline. What's more, it must be realized that these days a majority of concert engagements are likely to be staged at colleges and universities. And increasingly this leads to classroom discussion and demonstration and other contacts, more or less social and intellectual, in which musical virtuosity simply isn't enough: articulation must be transposed from the fingers to the tongue. Beyond these requirements are the day-to-day demands far from the glamour and the relative shelter of the platform. Whoever knows these things and has prepared himself accordingly, whoever can honestly and confidently claim that he is a talented, intelligent, knowledgeable musician, an efficient sight-reader, should be able to walk into a top job in a top orchestra at a top salary, whatever his race or color or creed.

Don't let anyone tell you that he has been trying to get an orchestral job for years and that he has been turned down consistently through "prejudice" or "favoritism" of some sort. The 1969 opening of the New York Philharmonic was marred by this sign-of-the-times item reported by the *Times:*

"Outside the hall . . . pickets of the Concerned Musicians Association paraded and passed out leaflets calling on the Philharmonic to hire more black musicians."

"Help us give black musicians a chance and black music students hope," a pamphlet urged. The Philharmonic has one Negro, a violinist hired eight years ago. Inside, patrons were handed a statement by Amyas Ames, then president of the orchestra, which said the Philharmonic had scorn for distinctions of race, color, and creed. There is a shortage of excellent musicians, the statement continued, and "we welcome all qualified candidates for any opening and seek help in finding them."

There you have it. The musical world finds itself in the same dilemma as all other professional worlds: torn between emotional reaction against racial prejudice and objective artistic standards.

This is a time for particular care and thought and honesty with ourselves, for racism of any sort corrupts art and destroys ideals no less than it wrecks whatever it touches. Bigotry is racist. So is the double standard in art. But few well-intentioned professionals have been free from prejudice. I plead guilty immediately though it emerges in reverse. Time and again, sitting on contest juries, admission boards, and managerial auditions, I have bent over backwards in misguided guilt, in overcompensation for generations of cruel social discrimination, to offer encouragement and opportunity to black musicians by lowering artistic standards that I uphold firmly toward white musicians.

In my heart of hearts I know full well that this is fundamentally wrong, esthetically and morally. Yet all of us today are under pressures from without and from within, to lower racial barriers. The same pressures, I am certain, lay behind the incredible choice of the all-black *No Place To Be Somebody* as a Pulitzer Prize play. Still, in this cockeyed moment of compromise, such pressures seem to me more tolerable than others that have made certain prizes reliable barometers of contemporary mediocrity.

Lowered standards are unfair to black artists, whom we owe the minimal compliment of treating as artists, not as black artists who deserve an extra "break" over other artists. Standards are standards. To forego them for any reason is an insult. For reasons of color, it is racism in reverse. Truly gifted blacks are all too aware of this, and each day on campus, in contest and concert, more black artists are appearing who are devotedly applying their minds and fingers to attain parity along with mastery.

Black or white or blue, a top artist can command any top job. A lesser artist has to accept a lesser job. A musician who is poorly equipped has little chance of getting or holding any job as a professional performer. Is this because of the higher standards stimulated by the "cultural explosion"? Not at all, for this rosy myth has been shown authoritatively to be little more than a statistical concoction.

In a comprehensive study of the *Economic Dilemma of the Performing Arts* issued in 1966, Professors William J. Baumol and William G. Bowen peel away layer after layer of euphoric illusion as to how many of us are going to concerts (as against ball games, for example), finding that the only substantial boom in the arts is taking place on campus. That particular boom is of course encouraging, but it scarcely touches the fact that community orchestras, opera-producing groups, and other essentially amateur activities around the country continue to keep afloat only through great personal sacrifices on the part of their organizers and performers.

Second, the effect of recordings, films, radio, and television has been as catastrophic professionally as it has been beneficial culturally in bringing fine music splendidly performed to remote areas. A single performance of a single musician or a single group can now be distributed and repeated at will, to an unlimited audience. Long gone are the days of employment for competent musicians in hotels, restaurants, and cinemas. Thirty years ago in this country, there were thirteen thousand movie houses with pit orchestras! And today, ironically, when an

47

orchestra or a soloist does manage to find a live audience, the performances may be dismissed out of hand because they don't stack up against those Philadelphia Orchestra albums or the Rubinstein and Heifetz disks on the shelf at home.

If there is any consolation in all of this, it is that a lot of live music is being staged these days, even though it has to fight tidal waves of competition—television, radio, recordings, ever better films and film scores. The overwhelming proportion of the live stuff is offered for free or for little, self-subsidized by musicians and musical groups. And when its producers and performers were shown by the 1965 Rockefeller Panel Report, *The Performing Arts: Problems and Prospects,* to be suffering from acute anemia, a large number of organizations and individuals became alarmed enough to examine the patient more carefully and concernedly.

That's one of the things I'm trying to do, but the patient keeps jumping out of bed. Recently, a jazz group using rock, electronics, and aleatory techniques, and the New York Pro Musica with a Gregorian singing ensemble had at each other on the same platform and program! It was such a smash sell-out that another concert was immediately announced, and the devil take the hindmost. Meanwhile—foundational subsidies, municipal-state-federal support, orchestral and operatic administrators, have all been feeding our patient vitamins. If everybody doesn't go broke and have to fold, he and we might muddle through somehow. As to when and how—your guess is as good as mine.

In this crazy "business" no one dares to generalize or prophesy (except authors in early chapters of books like this). Almost everything about the economics of art, especially musical art, makes us wiser only after the fact. This is a time to be less dogmatic, less blandly optimistic or dourly pessimistic about the future.

The time appears to be wide open, a time of transient fads and of timid recoiling, but also of forceful wrenching of old habits of thought and feeling, a time when we may be compelled to take on almost impossible odds, desperate odds, whether or not we can afford them.

Training the Musical Lion (and less sovereign beasts of the musical jungle)

The skills needed to meet today's performance standards (not to mention tomorrow's) are of such an altitude that one either starts the dizzy ascent early in life or not at all. No other period in history has demanded of the performer so many and varied qualifications in order to measure up to what the Greeks called the "complete" man.

Tomorrow's artist must also be a responsible and involved citizen. Long before he reaches his undergraduate or even his high school studies, a gifted youngster and his parents must begin learning how to develop his character as well as his talent so as to keep afloat in the uncharted seas ahead. And that, among other things, requires teachers whose specialties are supported by worldly interest and awareness.

The chief cause of high casualties among music students is the plethora of ignorant lesson peddlers who call themselves teachers. The steady trail of children in and out of their studios who wind up hating music is possible only because parents don't care enough or don't know enough to recognize either the presence of musicianship or the ability to teach. The surest way to kill a child's curiosity and potential in any endeavor is to subject him to bad teaching.

But what about the parent who does care but doesn't know? As with any other specialized field, a parent should seek out expert and unbiased advice. What if that seems impossible to find? Today this would appear highly unlikely, but I suppose the situation could arise. In that event, I would look for a teacher with lots of love and the desire to share it. By that I mean love for teaching, love for learning, and love for music—for all kinds and forms of music.

Look for a teacher who inspires not only love, but also wide interests, from pre-Bach motets to rock oratorios. Look for a teacher with a command of

51

his instrument, with a knowledge of its literature, and at least some acquaintance with others; one with patience, and—far from least—with a sense of humor. Seek out a teacher who instead of swamping pupils with routine will encourage them to invent their own exercises, improvise on tunes that intrigue them, compose their own, and learn the fascinating and invaluable games of reading all the clefs and of transposing anything into any key.

The private teaching vs. conservatory question seems to me a moot one, since each has its own distinct advantages. If a good music school is accessible, it will very likely offer group spirit and an element of competition, as well as membership in various combos—all valuable because young people can learn from each other as well as from teachers. Further, classes in harmony, composition, and other theoretical subjects are available and perhaps required. All of this should encourage not only technical proficiency but also communicative maturity. And with maturity might come, hopefully, the ability to interpret and illumine a work uniquely—a consummation as admirable today as it is rare. The process takes time: time for the teacher, time for the student. However, this very abundance of musical activity on the conservatory schedule—classes, lessons, concerts, practice sessions—works against the full opportunity to grow as a complete, creative human being, to learn that which is at the heart of all true education: how to teach oneself.

Studying with a private teacher during a student's high school years does not, as a rule, offer those disciplines in which conservatories specialize. Yet a fine teacher, free of the demands of an inflexible schedule, possessed of superior instrumental and intellectual accomplishments, can develop teenagers and enlarge their horizons in many vital ways that regimented schedules so often and sadly preclude. For example, there are the many details of speech, fashion, carriage, and etiquette, all of which for better or worse bear upon a performer's public image. But far more important, there is that warm, intimate, time-stopping involvement with ideas and books and records, with whatever or whoever enriches the moment. Where and how and when can any of this happen under the ruthless tyranny of the school bell?

The lack of this human dimension may be an imposition not only of academic routine but also of curricular narrowness. In art, a thorough understanding of the past is imperative for the continuance of high standards in the present. Performers and performances of the past are all but unknown to students who are not exposed to them either through a teacher's experience or through recordings. How many conservatories or universities have "urtexts" in their libraries or have on their faculties teachers who know and can demonstrate performance practices of the past? How many institutions have and make available the recordings of great performers no longer playing or no longer alive? And how many students are sufficiently aware, not to mention prepared, to come to terms with the belated proof—against a whole century of educational, editorial, and performing malpractice—that the musical world, with but a handful of shining exceptions, is still in the dark ages regarding the literature of the seventeenth and eighteenth centuries that include Bach, Handel, Haydn, and Mozart?

But little or no change will come unless enough deans of fine arts departments and chairmen of music departments feel secure enough to open their doors to those remaining scholars and artists who are capable of reviving and maintaining many near-lost traditions. The first faltering steps must help the mistaught to unlearn much that they now accept as gospel. Otherwise, the universities and conservatories—excepting a very few—must bear the blame before history of letting treasurable standards give way to appallingly inadequate performance and scholarship.

Yet if the conservatories fail to conserve great precedents, if the universities fail to resolve esthetic confrontations, and if both are "protecting" their students (and themselves, first and foremost) against the unsettled and unsettling professional facts of the present, they are failing utterly in their responsibility.

That music is a mercilessly exacting art is well known to musicians and non-musicians alike. That it is also a ruthlessly illogical business is little known except to the purveyors of its personalities and products. To many musicians themselves it is news that music is a business; and so is the fact that within its vast opportunities the capricious laws of chance play as decisive a role as the law of supply and demand—especially where soloists are concerned.

The system whereby the best, hopefully, goes to the top and the worst sinks to the bottom becomes too often in the music field what we might call, to paraphrase Darwin, "the survival of the slickest." On the one hand are those case histories of remarkably talented and finely equipped soloists who, with all their mastery, have been unable to earn a living. On the other are a corresponding number of "the slickest"—performers who are somehow always with us, and not only surviving but reaping substantial rewards.

Now, justice of a kind is beginning to catch up. The dizzy pace of the times has escalated the standards of sheer skill needed to attain and maintain success in today's concert jungle. The "slick" have as tough a time as the solidly equipped.

These dreary observations in a chapter on training underline one of the few certainties in any professional music career today: the necessity to arm oneself in every conceivable way against the *un*certainties. Regardless of the ever-increasing opportunities open to all but the solo musician, no one should attempt to fill them without adequate talent and training. And the higher the ambitions, the higher are the required levels of technical prowess before there is the ghost of a chance of realizing them.

This may seem like repetitious finger-wagging, but experience shows that there is scarcely a more innocent group, a less realistic group of talented people than classical musicians. The average newsboy plans his work with more precision, more practical intelligence than the average would-be professional musician, whether the musician's aim is stardom, or the more modest yet equally significant goals of ensemble or orchestral playing, accompanying, and so on.

This is the more curious because of the unpalatable fact that music is still a luxury in our society; that artists are at the mercy of an inconstant public divided in its patronage between entertainment and the daily necessities, which include medical and legal services. Yet the students of *those* professions, in common with other indispensable workers, face the problems of apprenticeship, of adequate internship, and of eventual employment with a realism and an appetite for guidance that today's musician too often considers beneath his dignity. Too few students understand that the basic problems of music as a career are identical with those of any other artistic or business career.

Every product—and this certainly includes artistic products—has to be created, distributed, and bought. Although the primary factors of performance are the program, the interpreter, and the audience, the successful of the musical world are made through a combination of gifts and circumstances *only partly musical*. Essentially, the great box office attractions have been personalities who have recognized that practical issues are as important to a public career as are artistic ideals and abilities. The nonprofit managements that we shall discuss in a later chapter are most valuable to the extent that they give their charges on-the-job training in business acumen, public relations, stage deportment, and certain other "fringe" aspects of a successful career. In later chapters, we shall touch upon other requirements, beyond traditional musicianship, imposed by today's rapidly evolving society.

In any field, rare is the individual who knows what

is knowable about his work and drives equally hard at each aspect of it. Most people are less than equal to their tasks, especially in the study of music. The most common hazards are depending too heavily upon innate gifts, underestimating the need for intensive study and work, and neglecting to develop one's mind and personality both on and off the platform. *There is no more important talent than the gift for using talent.*

Almost as harmful to a career as ignorance or self-containment is haste. Although there are isolated cases of instant success, musical stardom is usually achieved slowly, after long periods of patient application and preparation. These alone enable a young artist to turn to long-term account the "golden opportunity" should it arise. Most often, big successes—even apparently "instant" ones—have emerged from a series of modest occasions, which have been utilized with the kind of acuteness that parts the heaviest portals.

Neither the extent nor the speed of an artist's public recognition are accurate measures of his talents. The slow climb that led to fame and fortune for such undeniable instrumental geniuses as Fritz Kreisler, Ignace Paderewski, and Artur Rubinstein could be further illustrated by many artists who endured years of public apathy before they became popular favorites.

Was this because they were not known as child prodigies? On the contrary, most great artists were extremely precocious, some from infancy. Most of those whose precocity was prematurely exploited never survived to fulfill their promise. In the words of the witty Leopold Godowsky, "In most wonder-children, the wonder disappears and only the child remains." A century ago Franz Liszt said, "As a child, I was exposed to public criticism as a prodigy, through the ignorance of my parents, long before I was properly prepared to meet the inevitable consequences of public appearance. This was an incalculable injury to me."

At this writing a case in point of a pianist who appears to be carefully avoiding such injury is that of young André Watts, who was shot into prominence a few years ago when Leonard Bernstein championed him at the age of sixteen. His stunning pinch-hit performance of the Liszt *E-flat Concerto* for the ailing Glenn Gould brought with it all the makings of instant success. Yet at Bernstein's strong recommendation, he continued his piano studies with Genia Robinor at the Philadelphia prep school he was attending. Roy Cusumano, the teacher who rescheduled a history exam that year so that André could keep what he modestly called an "appointment" in New York, has described his close view of the young virtuoso:

"He told me once that if he did possess the talent to reach the top, he was in no hurry to get there. Many young artists attempt to become great too soon. By forcing their gift, they ruin it. André did not wish to add his name to that list of forgotten prodigies. His plan was to go patiently and carefully through the phases of learning his craft and to be fully prepared for success.

"Recently, André has been studying with Leon Fleisher as he works for his Bachelor of Music degree at the Peabody Conservatory in Baltimore, and for the past several years since his prep school days, he has earned a reputation of mammoth proportions through limited national and international concert tours. . . ."

In the United States, we are now in a relatively fortunate position. Talent is everywhere and, increasingly, so is the realization that talent alone is not enough. In addition, most professional musicians, no matter what their specialization, recognize music education as a high and separate art. The day that most first-class composers, conductors, performers, and musicologists truly involve themselves at all levels of education, from preschool through university, will mark our musical millennium. Meanwhile, their dedication has already initiated the interrelation of all music study, and has resulted in an extended and improved program of music instruction, which, despite its obvious and inevitable shortcomings in meeting contemporary requirements, is still second to that of no other country.

Not long ago, exceptional teaching was available only in the largest population centers. Today, in any number of large and small communities throughout the nation, many fine musicians and educators are playing leading roles in local musical life, performing in symphonies and bands, and teaching in colleges, universities, and conservatories. The latter, along with private studios, have traditionally produced the great majority of star performers. But now there are few conservatories worthy of the name that aren't linked somehow with a university, which not only can bring to the conservatory student a balanced curriculum but can also bless him with a degree. And a degree may be a step toward greater career security—if perhaps less income —than stardom itself.

The first-rate conservatories are still the "specialists," with all the assets that the potential star requires: the best teachers, the finest facilities in all fields of performing art, the constant opportunity to hear and be heard, the steady stimulation of exposure to musical versatility and stylistic experimentation, where string quartets, jazz combos or opera groups are equally available.

The solo-minded student must therefore head for

the perfectionist environment of the best conservatories for a full-time encounter with creative people
and big-league standards. In the purely academic
environment of a university, no matter how art-ori-
ented, too much time and effort and energy are con-
sumed by the usual and sometimes irrelevant
demands of the curriculum.

As for the high cost of learning, truly gifted people who belong in music will have little difficulty
today in getting full scholarships at the finest conservatories. The exceptional talents will not lack for
actual support from subsidies, loans, and grants. And
should additional aid be needed to span the gap
between advanced study and the professional plunge,
anything from baby-sitting to accompanying or
coaching could profitably take the place of the court
patronage of yore or of the government subsidy on
which most European students of talent can depend.
It should be noted, however, that despite the lack
of state, municipal, and federal support of the arts
in the United States, the dream of most foreign
music students is to study and work in America.

It may be significant that certain university music
schools have moved towards conservatory status, as
witness the appointment of quite a few of the foremost performing artists to the staffs of academic institutions. As far back as thirty years ago, Egon
Petri was artist-in-residence at Cornell. A decade

later, Robert Casadesus was at Princeton, and a decade after that spectacularly placed on the campus of
the University of Southern California were violinist Jascha Heifetz, cellist Gregor Piatigorsky, and
violist William Primrose.

Today, we find distinguished instrumentalists
such as Abbey Simon, Sydney Foster, Jorge Bolet,
and Joseph Gingold at the University of Indiana;
Lili Kraus at Texas Christian University; Ozan
Marsh and baritone Igor Gorin at the University of
Arizona; Gunnar Johansen at the University of Wisconsin. At the University of Cincinnati, there is not
only Raymond Dudley on the faculty, but also the
hyphenated name that exalts a musical institution
to "College-Conservatory of Music."

And yesterday, our Ivy League institutions welcomed such creative individuals as Walter Piston at
Harvard, Roger Sessions at Princeton, Quincy Porter
at Yale, and Douglas Moore at Columbia, whose
first musical head was Edward MacDowell.

Now, having acknowledged the high standards of
the artistic personnel of a modicum among our
fourteen hundred institutions of higher learning, it
would appear logical to conclude that they offer
students (other than the would-be soloist, for whom
the conservatory is indicated), the most promising
training.

Yes and no. The most versatile training, yes, but

without a new approach geared to the full development of those who aspire to artistic and technical mastery, a thousand times no.

Soloists comprise the smallest segment of an enormous field. More indispensable to our whole musical life are competently equipped teachers, conductors, ensemble and orchestra players, accompanists, music educators, researchers, librarians. The list must also include contributors to such allied fields as broadcasting, motion pictures, recordings, publishing, selling, managing—not to mention administering, among other things, our precocious and ailing cultural centers with the help of musical therapists!

In these areas, the universities for all their deficiencies are doing whatever they can for the most people. However, in this time of battle on campus for a new order, musically gifted youngsters may have to mount and sustain some kind of attack on the remaining strongholds of encrusted academicism, in order to gain a musical education that is relevant to their time, that can bear on their own needs and future. Though most of today's musical institutions are to some degree old-fangled, it is to their credit that more and more of them have, for instance, been engaging pop musicians who have vitalized departments of theory and harmony and composition by extending their horizons and their idioms. Partly through this influence, our Europe-oriented methods and materials and goals have begun to make room for Asia and Africa, for the West and East Indies, for the fusion of folk and art materials.

The need for this reorientation reaches down to the broad base of music education in primary and secondary schools. Harris Danziger, presiding at the National Guild of Community Music Schools, said at the guild's 1968 convention in Los Angeles: "The response of serious music education to the inclusion of Spanish and Afro-American elements into our musical speech will determine in large measure its continued vitality." He went on to advise against any superficial, patchwork implementation of this response, which would accept only those changes compatible with present subjects and disciplines.

One fairly widespread change on the conservatory level is a restudying of the most characteristic element of jazz, improvisation. As a result, a fresh and almost forgotten environment of Baroque creativity is being returned to the classical musician. The reemergence of this invaluable skill is destined to have a profound effect upon the performing artist of tomorrow. Aleatorical skills are in great demand today even in orchestral playing, and the interpreter who can't improvise on the spot may find himself seriously handicapped. In this whole area of spontaneity in performance, the so-called classical artists have been embarrassingly outclassed by their pop brethren—mainly because of the two different worlds of teaching involved. Unquestionably, many aspects of musical training must be re-examined on all levels if students are to survive, let alone flourish, in the rapidly changing social, economic, and artistic conditions of our hectic era.

One of these aspects, discussed elsewhere, is the versatility which the average musician must acquire if he is not to be profoundly hindered. Yet in seeming defiance of this need, there are those who cannot be all things to all music and have made exceptionally fine careers and contributions by becoming specialists. I once ventured the opinion that a specialist is one who does everything else worse; but I was then talking about those who worked to gain reputations as specialists merely by narrowing down to "nothing but." I was not talking of such extraordinary examples as pianist Artur Schnabel in Beethoven, harpsichordist Wanda Landowska in the Baroque literature, pianist Walter Gieseking in French Impressionism, or young violinist Paul Zukovsky in the bramble patch of the avant garde. Artists of this caliber are a boon to whatever composer or other enthusiasm transforms them into loving disciples and living symbols. In the process, most of them have won special distinction as well as public esteem.

But never can this happen through a conscious *determination* to specialize. Affinity for the material —emotional, intellectual, and spiritual—is what makes for convincing communication, whether or not it is expressed in a particular speciality. "Always pick out music that talks to you," said Josef Hofmann. "You must feel this about everything that you play before audiences, if you would communicate with them."

Hofmann was careful to say that such selectivity should apply to music played "before audiences." No musician realized better than he how many works a great artist must *know* beyond those relatively few he has time to *learn*—including many works in literatures other than his own. Without a score, Artur Rubinstein can sit down and play the orchestral parts of the most important violin and cello concertos, the piano parts of the most significant chamber works, and the scores of many operas —of which he sings every aria and every word!

This, along with regular performance preparation, takes a lot of "armchair practice" away from an instrument. Once, while riding in a train to Berlin with Josef Hofmann, I turned to say something to him. He put up a restraining hand and shook his head from side to side, saying, "Excuse me, please, I'm practicing." The student should early develop this faculty, and so add greatly to his available time for study, memorization, and practice. Mental rehearsal, furthermore, saves physical fatigue and accomplishes what no amount of muscular and mechanical practice could possibly attain.

To master it to the degree that Hofmann did requires not only concentrated thought, not only talent, but something of what we call genius. Can anything short of genius, actually, hope to reach success in a solo career? Should anything short of genius tackle the total discipline of conservatory training? We can't really answer these questions until we find out more about determining and measuring talent or genius, but much can be discovered about these elusive things from observation.

Carlyle's famous definition of genius as "the transcendent capacity for taking trouble first of all" was ridiculed by Herbert Spencer, who insisted that genius is in fact diametrically opposite, being the ability to do with little or no trouble what could never be done by a less gifted person—no matter how much trouble he took.

Yet whether or not "taking trouble" *is* genius, geniuses who never took the trouble to prove their right to the term with training, knowledge, and discipline are as common as they are tragic. "Without the most devotional application," said Henry L. Mencken, "talent, and even genius, is impotent. The talented in any field with equal powers of application and concentration—he is the one who most often has left his mark upon the world."

A peculiarly American factor of *failure* in training has already received some attention in this chapter, but I believe it deserves further emphasis here. Theodor Leschetizky, the great piano teacher, once said, "The Americans have amazing powers of acquiring knowledge. In that way they are my best pupils. But their main fault is their extreme hurry. They come to Europe in a hurry, they want to learn everything in a hurry, and they return home in a hurry. That is the curse of art. In business it may mean progress. In music, it means superficiality."

It is invariably the most gifted who are also the most ambitious, the most anxious, the most intense, and hence—with an occasional exception like André Watts—the most impatient. It takes time, a lifetime maybe, to explore that elusive thing called talent, which is not one but many things. Each component of talent may not only vary widely from the others but may be present in any given case to a merely ordinary degree—or not at all.

Sometimes, the apparent absence of one facet of a talent has been traceable to the study of a "wrong instrument." But most frequently we find talent broken up into compartments. A musician may have a naturally beautiful tone, absolute pitch, and a fine memory, but little muscular coordination. He may have a phenomenal, "inborn" mechanical facility, yet be a slow reader or learner. He may have just about "everything" to a remarkable degree and yet fall apart through nervousness before an audience. He may have an overwhelming dramatic drive and yet be insufficiently master of himself to project to a public. Ergo, the potentials, pitfalls, and partitions of a talent need to be recognized early in its development; the good teacher will know which aspects to cultivate and which to prune in the pursuit of completeness.

The reader may be wondering why a chapter ostensibly devoted to the process of training should say so little about its day-to-day particulars. Where are the lists of entrance requirements, curricular offerings, available certificates and degrees? They are, of course, in the catalogues of the conservatories and music schools, and may be had at the drop of a postcard. My concern, in this chapter and the next, is with what is *not* in those catalogues—or is at best tucked well in between the lines. The facts of professional life are so rigorously selective today for the solo performer that any merely academic or repertorial approach to his training is more than ever before an unrealistic one.

This is what impels me—as also in the discussions of management and contests elsewhere in the book —to emphasize the larger human guidelines rather than the narrower curricular ones. It is my hope that the reader with professional goals may then evaluate his candidacy not so much for an institution as for a way of life. Without such an orientation, years of specialized study might be wasted.

The student's talent, in other words, had better not just be a talent for an instrument, but also— no less important—a talent for music, for patient work, for self-discipline. And today especially, a talent for living, learning, and loving—to the hilt.

Then it becomes the job of the teacher and the institution to recognize, nurture, and strengthen those talents and tendencies, to direct them toward their fullest completeness, to prepare the student for the fiery trials ahead.

And when the musician, having absorbed all available instruction, training, and experience, stands undissuaded on the brink of a career, with no assurance that in five years any public at all in the traditional sense will be awaiting him—what then?

Technique and more technique, experience and more experience, trying anything and everything time and again, playing whenever, wherever he can, and for whomever he can. The aristocratic Paderewski once said, "Invite your garbage man to hear

71

you. If he will listen, play for him as much as you can. If he will give you his honest reaction, so much the better."

In the non-soloist field, top-drawer orchestral and conductorial experience is available throughout the country, even in the toughest of all towns. In New York City, there is the National Orchestral Association, initiated by Leon Barzin, one of the few made-in-the-U.S.A. conductors of the first rank. The 1970 season marked four decades of unique service to the music and musicians of our country and was touched off by bold and expanded plans, more fellowships and more concerts to enable players and conductors to complete their educational work under professional conditions, firmly guided by Barnett Byman.

Also in the big town, but on a completely professional level, is the American Symphony, which reflects conductor Leopold Stokowski's love for young people and respect for the instrumental talent of women. This remarkable orchestra is full of brilliantly gifted and finely equipped youngsters, and the entire musical world relishes the quip that "there are forty-two women in Stokie's hundred-man orchestra."

The talented young musician who has worked hard and utilized the chances to develop his gifts and personality, eventually must arm himself psychologically for the inevitable decision: whether to

TRAINING THE MUSICAL LION

shoot for the highest stakes as a soloist via the contest route or any other path that opens up, or to
settle for the more accessible, more numerous, and
far more secure possibilities on less rarified levels.

It may be customary and comforting to conclude
this sort of chapter with a bracing reminder that the
musical world is an enormous one with a place in it
for whoever has what it takes. And even if he has
some rough times, at least he is doing something he
loves to do, and there is nothing better than that.

I'm not so sure. I think that far more objective
standards and self-assessment are required for survival in the musical jungle, and that we've got to be
mighty careful what it is we want in music as in
life—precisely because we're so apt to get it.

The University:
Haven or Battleground?

*T*ime was when the university provided an ivy-covered retreat, a sequestered haven where the scholar—if not, as a rule, the artist—could find a safe world in which to live, meet with his classes, and do his work. Any rowdiness, any letting off of steam, usually appeared as part of some tradition, fraternal or otherwise. Musicologists could join the faculty to teach a little history, theory, "appreciation," and to encourage a little extracurricular sing-

74

ing, scraping, or tootling. A few professional performers appeared on a respectfully but sparsely attended concert series. Students looking toward a music career either went to a conservatory, or "broadened" themselves at a university, where they marked time for four years.

As this is being written, most of the ivy is still around, except where it's been torn off by students climbing in and out of windows with food for their embattled chums holding a building under siege. In other ways, though, the old place has changed not a little. "Retreat" is no longer the word that comes first to mind. Tradition in all phases of university life has been unceremoniously overturned.

And what about the young career-minded musician? Part of the change on campus, since long before the first disturbances, has been in his favor. The titles of "artist-in-residence" and, more recently, "affiliate artist" have become familiar. The former category, including composers, pianists, violinists, singers, and occasionally other musicians, applies to those who are engaged throughout the teaching season as members of the faculty, and are permitted to accept outside concert engagements. The latter category applies to a newer relationship between artist and institution, sponsored in the main by Affiliate Artist, Inc., a nonprofit organization in New York.

This provides a flexible arrangement that allows an artist to be utilized on campus for short periods of time in any way he might be needed, usually from two weeks to two months per year on a three-year contract.

A more or less typical affiliate's schedule, that of baritone Richard Allen at Gustavus Adolphus College in St. Peter, Minnesota, was reported as follows in the *New York Times*:

> Sang music by Schütz at choral vespers on Saturday; took part in Reformation Sunday services; held informal talks with students for three days and lectured to an alumni group; gave a lecture-song-demonstration (known variously as "talk-sing" or "LSD") on the relationship of French impressionist poetry, painting, and music. [Allen had been a Fulbright scholar in France, a pupil of Pierre Bernac, a teacher of French in New York high schools]; rehearsed and sang with orchestra a Bach cantata; gave a talk-sing on opera in English and its demands on the American singer; drove six students to Minneapolis for a performance of *The Barber of Seville* by the Goldovsky Opera Company [Allen was once a member and could provide a backstage tour]; and so on.

A pianist or violinist might not manage quite this variety, but with imagination and cooperation he could come close to it.

The gradualness of such innovations is not hard to understand, even in institutions where other changes are now being pushed more abruptly, to put it gently. The main emphasis in American public education has been and still is a vocational one intended to steer students toward economic security. From this point of view, the study of the arts has been considered virtually valueless, and the possibility of an artistic career yielding any practical result was slight at best. As for studying the arts as a discipline to sharpen perception or strengthen the spiritual and moral capacity to handle life's problems—that was way beyond the public ken.

Yet, each day we get further away from the provincial attitude that the arts are merely a diversion or a frill. Even public education is beginning to contemplate in a gingerly way the inclusion of music as a core element of the curriculum. One of these years it may become normal for a musically inclined high school graduate to approach a college, university, or conservatory with a reasonably solid grounding in the language of music, if not its history. Hardly five per cent fit that description now, but for those who do, the best of the universities today, with all their abrasions and uncertainties,

77

are still a good place to be. A few universities already boast music schools easily as strong in faculty and curriculum as an average conservatory. And they also offer a provocative academic environment denied the usual conservatory or, to an extent, the college, with opportunities for both formal and informal, curricular and extracurricular correlations between music and the other disciplines.

Such universities, it must be emphasized, are not recommended to the student who will settle only for a solo career. He needs the full professional concentration of such specialized conservatories as the Curtis Institute of Music in Philadelphia, the Juilliard, Manhattan and Mannes schools in New York, the Cleveland Institute, the Chicago College of Music, the Peabody Conservatory in Baltimore, and the Eastman School in Rochester.

A formidable group. Yet, the exacting George Szell, while preferring the "best" American conservatories over their counterparts abroad, insisted on limiting the comparison to the best. "The others, with perhaps an exception here and there, musically and intellectually are apt to be pretty insipid. Perhaps it's partially the fault of pressures, the temptation or necessity to make quick careers, to try to turn instantly into money whatever one can do, no matter how. There's nothing so important for people who want to do well to realize as soon as possible the need for strong and solid preparation, for an all-around equipment. Everyone's in such a hurry—that's the weak link in American *conservatory* training. The profound elements—reflection, depth, imagination—are all better understood in American *universities.*"

Certainly colleges and universities have come a long way since composer Randall Thompson, on an inspection tour in the early 1940s, found what he termed "a typical and appalling instructor" using Leopold Stokowski's sumptuous transcription of Bach's organ *Passacaglia and Fugue* as "an illuminating example" of Baroque orchestration! The pendulum invariably swings and today, generally, one finds university music curricula overweighted with theory, history, and musicology as against applied composing, conducting, and performing. Consequently, the creative and interpretive drives are often damaged or dispersed by conflicting academic demands.

This becomes no less a frustration for the teacher than for the student. The term "in residence," with its overtones of serenity and leisure for a creator or an interpreter, can serve as window-dressing for a full load of chores, complete with mandatory conferences and committee memberships to a point where self-expression is suffocated. But the realist should know that, in this life, we must anticipate paying a price for everything, though we may complain that it's just too damned high—sometimes insufferably so.

Gardner Read, composer-in-residence at Boston University, wrote in the *Music Journal:* "Artists-in-residence may have been appointed to their posts because of their publicity value as composers, as writers, or as painters, but when it comes to such matters as salary, schedule, rank, teaching load, and even tenure, the questions from dean or department chairman are: 'Is he effective in the classroom?' and 'Did he do a good job on the library committee?' and unfortunately not: 'Did you read the superb reviews of his new historical novel in *The New York Times* and *Saturday Review?'* Or the raves they gave his last disk or concert?"

In spite of such problems—and Mr. Read is admittedly not describing the best aspects of the pedagogical post for the artist—a surprising number of faculty musicians (including his distinguished and productive self) do manage to combine academic duties with prolific activities, as composers, as solo performers, in local orchestras, or even in jazz combos. The latter appears to be especially engaging to students, for whom such worldly versatility is the ultimate in sophistication.

As the myth of the "cultural explosion" lies exploded at our feet, it should not be too astonishing to find that college and university campuses represent the one area of our national life where some actual cultural expansion *is* going on, where the idea of nurturing art is implanted. Not necessarily, of course, in the Beethoven-Shakespeare-Rembrandt sense that for many lies at the center of art, but more likely in terms of galvanic activity and exposure, involving media that may not only be electronic but cyclonic, not only mixed but mashed. In Michigan, the university celebrated its ninetieth concert season in 1969 with attractions that ranged from the latest hot combos to the Vienna Symphony and La Scala Opera company. A Columbia Management representative recently said, "The universities are the largest buyers of serious music today—to the tune of at least 75 per cent of the professional activity in the United States today, and it goes without saying that in the pop field the monopoly is complete."

It's true, of course, that the "democratization" of art has for the moment, at least, undermined its unique power to inculcate the highest standards of excellence. Yet the previous efforts to promote familiarity with art—too often as a status symbol —encouraged the presentation of masterpieces in the deadly form of "it's-good-for-you" culture rather than as the thrilling experiences they can be.

When we face these realities, it becomes even

81

more heartening to see our universities maintaining a protective attitude toward creative and interpretive artists and scholars. In the tradition of princely art patrons of the past, they enable many artists to do their work in comparative serenity and safety, to experiment as free spirits, and to attract selective and receptive audiences.

Even in the far-out field of electronic music, the universities, following the example of the Columbia-Princeton Electronic Music Center in New York, are the logical places to install the expensive and intricate equipment required. The many uses to which the new aural materials are being put, in television, radio, movies, and now in special concerts, offer numerous opportunities for a host of new composers and performers. Built around the highly personal, original, and powerful professional nucleus which has existed within it from its beginning, this development has taken firmer hold here than in Europe; and partly because of it the decade of the 1960s became the most revolutionary period in the annals of American music.

The university and college audiences for the "new sounds" in classical music; the mobs that crowd the pads and palaces of rock; and finally church services and jazz-rock masses and liturgical "conferences" characterized by heavily attended, unorthodox ceremonies, by priests and nuns rocking in serpentine lines while psychedelic lights throw eerie patterns on ceiling and seats—these are portents of things to come, and things to go.

It is symptomatic of the times that one can speak in almost the same breath of the university as a part-time haven for the artist and as the scene of such esthetic and pseudo-esthetic happenings as these. It is also symptomatic that, in student communities, the majority is turning to art as entertainment for the most comfortable possible experience, while the minority is turning to it as a kind of religious asceticism for the most *un*comfortable. Today the same elements of protest and confrontation, the same "generation gap" that has threatened or weakened the traditional security of all areas of life, exist with special concentration in the arts. While at their best these elements stir healthy innovation, they also play havoc with the dying Establishment.

The urgent need, more often than not, is the familiar one of communication—an ironic one in this age of hyper-mass-communications. Certain of the younger and more youth-related concert managers have made sterling efforts to bridge the gap between tradition—hardly the "in" thing these days—and innovation. Manager Ann Summers, for instance, tells of an appraisal of concert management she led before an audience of three hundred students and faculty at a New England university at which two-and-a-half rival concert courses existed; the first was twenty years old, a sparsely attended music-department series of recitals featuring visiting artists in standard literature; the second was five years old, a more adventurous series (including a brass quintet and some programs presenting unfamiliar instruments) run by the drama director; the "half" was a student-run series of rock-oriented events that often packed a much larger hall.

A managerial colleague who had come from New York with Mrs. Summers spoke first, and unwisely used the occasion to try and whip up enthusiasm for a forthcoming recital by a Metropolitan Opera soprano whose appearance, through ignorance or mere indifference, promised to attract less than a corporal's guard.

"Tell your friends about it. Make them come," he urged in his off-campus innocence.

"Why push your tastes on us? And why should we push our tastes on others?" were characteristic questions from students.

During the give and take, a faculty member complained how few students had been attending the faculty concerts. Another student asked, "How many of the faculty here have ever gone to *our* concerts?" Not one hand went up. But the hackles of the faculty member in question did, and he retorted angrily, "When I've finished my work after a long week, I don't feel I have to go out and hear that kind of garbage."

Up went the barriers, higher than ever, and he knew it. Floundering and flustered, he asked the last student, "Are you in any of my classes?"

"No sir, I'm not."

"Well, of course, then I'm at a disadvantage," said the teacher, looking sad and smiling feebly. The power play came through, loud and clear.

Taking her cue, Mrs. Summers arranged for a concert by the New York Jazz Sextet to be given some weeks later on the second series. Even here, it was a radical innovation, for it showed students, who packed the event to the rafters, how they too could improvise. The enthusiasm aroused was unprecedented.

A more recent visit to the same university by the veteran balladeer, Richard Dyer Bennet, pulled music and drama, the concert series and the curriculum itself, into a new cohesiveness. One day, for example, he wandered into a Shakespeare rehearsal. The students were limping through the lines without understanding, without pleasure or vigor. He showed them how to make speech sing, how to capture the mood and meanings of the inspiring text. The results and the excitement are difficult to describe. Mrs. Summers reports: "Doors were opened where there had been a reinforced concrete wall. From all sides came demands for Bennet's return."

This particular breakthrough speaks volumes about the cultural growing pains of the university today and, despite them, what *can* happen there; about the urgent gaps to be bridged between artists and academicians, between administration and faculty and student, between tradition and innovation, between what is essentially art and what is essentially entertainment; about the need to recognize in each case the mutual needs and the vast possibilities. Another step in the right direction, already taken here and there, is away from the enslavement of the full-dress strait jacket, away from the one-shot concert in some cultural crypt, featuring some weary war horse and/or some nerve-shattering novelty. This ritual has been among the most efficient ways of turning off a generation in search of freshness and vitality.

Perhaps, as well as training musicians and theoreticians, universities should initiate courses in concert management and presentation which would tackle the urgent question of audience reaction and audience development. It's not my idea. Right now, Herbert von Karajan is the voluntary subject for just such experiments being carried on abroad.

One thing we know, or ought to know. Concerts

today must be where the action is, where the façade is down, where spontaneity flows, and where the element of surprise keeps performances viable. Under such conditions, the university could come into its own as a free-spirited realm with no walls separating learning from living.

During the course of a pre-publication trip to a few major academic institutions, I made special inquiries to determine to what degree the music departments were aware of the need to broaden and to humanize the curriculum, and above all, to face the undeniable fact that our schools desperately require organic change. Two reactions—one from a music student, another from an artist-in-residence —are provocative enough to quote fully.

The student was a sophomore on a four-year music scholarship at an embattled university in southern California. When I asked about his music studies, he almost scowled as he said, "Are you kidding? What part of the music curriculum? The old-hat worship of the three Bs? The adulation of the electronic eunuchs? Learning the notes of a graduation program from Scarlatti to Stravinsky— the same one my piano prof's been dishing out for over twenty years? What's that got to do with life today? We're wondering if and when we'll be blown to bits by bombs, and what in hell to do about this terrible world."

87

"What are you doing here if you feel that way?" I asked.

"I'll tell you. I'm in the Free Speech Movement, SDS, and on the civil rights magazine staff. I'm learning confrontation tactics, how to duck tear gas canisters and like that. In music, we know we're getting a smattering of history and a lot of irrelevancies or lies called the rules of composition that apply only to their goddamn textbook exercises. After the first three months I was almost a drop-out, but then I got wise and decided to stay on long enough to get a bachelor's degree for free, and maybe a master's and maybe also keep out of the draft. That's it."

"Suppose you manage that," I said. "What are you planning to do with music?"

"Nothing that's directly related to the curriculum around here, except getting some kind of background I might use in some way. You see, my idea of musicians of our time is represented mainly by Dylan and the Beatles, by Ellington when he doesn't get fancy and 'symphonic,' Basie, the Modern Jazz Quartet, people like that, people who understand what we're feeling, who feel the same, and who are making an art out of what we're all feeling together."

"Exactly what is that?" I asked.

"It's not complicated," he said. "At the base of

it all are hopes and fears. We don't want to be killed and we don't want to kill. We don't want to murder women and old men and little kids. Next, this ecology thing has extended itself to the arts. They're doing the same thing with music as with everything else—it's been corrupted and commercialized and polluted until it stinks—almost all of the classical field, and a helluva lot of the pop field. Next—our rubber-mouthed university academicians and our politicians—even those who are honest and enlightened—they don't know how to cope and they are completely unable to teach us how to cope. They have failed. They know it, we know it, and they know we know. It's a wonder more of 'em don't take drugs."

The artist-teacher, with a gesture of despair, said, "Look, we're all doing our very best. The kids are very smart and some of them are talented and all of them and us too are trying to do what I'm afraid is the impossible. We can only help them to learn what we know about music, to get a serviceable technique on their major instrument and a certain facility on one or two more, to acquire the elements of a liberal education, and to encourage them to chart their own education and political courses more independently by taking part in policy-making at school, or by helping to make decisions in whatever governs their lives.

89

"Now, that's quite a job. We can assist them in it but only to the extent of our own abilities and possibilities. Right now, I feel frustrated and even guilty. Limitations of time make teaching too impersonal; limitations of my own education make me too inflexible, too authoritarian for a generation that has so much that is unorthodox and new to face when we push them out of here.

"As to helping them with the challenges of jazz, rock, electronics, computers, or recording, TV, film music—I'm sunk and so are most members of this department. We ourselves would need no less teaching, and much more time than our pupils if we wanted to tackle those problems. Hell, let's face it, what do we know even about the style and ornamental practices of seventeenth and eighteenth century music? Nothing. And when I suggested to the head of the music department that we ought to initiate a course in it, if we could get the right person to conduct it, he shook, he was terrified. In short, a lot of what's wrong here is due to sheer ignorance that tries to protect itself against exposure. I admit it. Quote me freely if it helps to improve the situation and I can remain anonymous."

Again the "blunt cool," as though I didn't know it.

Never again can the university be characterized, for the musician or for anyone else, as an ivy-covered haven. A retreat, perhaps. A hotbed, certainly. Above all, a good place to learn, to work, to fight one's own battles, as always. But also, surely, where art can be at the heart of life, where teachers and students may educate and inspire and nourish each other, if only they would. Then will the college campus be our brightest hope.

6

Contests:
The Only Game in Town

*I*n 1961, writing a supplementary chapter for *Speaking of Pianists*, I welcomed the emergence of the competition as a "magic catalyst," a new ingredient needed "to dramatize achievement so as to accelerate its recognition, development, and exploitation.

"From the moment that Van Cliburn's Moscow triumph caught us with our cultural sights down," I explained, "the stigma that was upon such tests of ability was forever dissolved. Formerly, whoever dared to enter a competition branded himself a student, not an artist. No matter how stringent the test, how esteemed the jury, how brilliant the winner's performance, the musical merchants and press and public remained, with few exceptions, stonily unresponsive. One fine artist after another, including Cliburn, had competed victoriously for the highest prizes of the finest competitions both here and abroad. But even when their victories initiated significant and successful engagements, most of them soon found themselves precisely where they were before—nowhere at all."

All this had been changed by the dramatic brush fire of the 1958 Tchaikovsky Competition, which sent Cliburn home a conquering hero of the cold war. The Leventritt Foundation, whose prizes had brought modest celebrity, if any, to its winners, began offering finalists a Carnegie Hall audience and, for its twentieth anniversary in 1959, major orchestral support. I mentioned Malcolm Frager's unprecedented seven-month passage that year from a first prize at the Leventritt to another one at the highly prestigious Queen Elisabeth Competition in Brussels. All this yielded money, orchestral engagements, and publicity. By every sign, the international competition was taking up the job of career-launching at a time when the New York debut recital had just about put it down. "Catalyst" seemed to be the word—at the time.

Not a few years have passed since all this happened. Competitions for instrumentalists have sprouted and grown almost everywhere, though the older ones still rule the pack: the Tchaikovsky, the Thibaud-Long, the Queen Elisabeth, the Leventritt, the Naumburg, the Busoni and the Chopin for pianists, the Paganini and the Wieniawski for violinists, the Casals for cellists. Two affluent newcomers are the Van Cliburn International Piano Competition in Texas, and the Montreal in Canada. Judging by all the activity, my optimism in 1961 might appear to have been well founded.

Actually, however, the very fact of proliferation has thinned out the effect of contests and gradually dulled their shine, and they have turned into a pretty ordinary game. Nevertheless, you might say that it's the only game in town.

No competition can assure an artist's career. The most it can do is to catapult him before the public. He will then probably find his way into the same sort of career (or lack of it) that, given the needed patience and determination, he would have found sooner or later without prizes. From Frager's sensational pair of wins, for instance, has come a rather quiet and unpretentious career. Yet the playing of this fine artist continues to mature, and to confirm the judges' decisions in New York and in Brussels.

Are careers without newsworthy prizes possible today? Certainly, though most likely with a boost from some other kind of rocket. Specialization may help, if it works as well as it has for Rosalyn Tureck with her devotion to Bach. Among younger contemporaries, the Frenchman Philippe Entremont has been lifted into a steady if again unsensational success by a string of recordings, cannily chosen and promoted. Daniel Barenboim, pianist and conducfor, and Jacqueline Du Pré, cellist, have married and are making music with immense flair and extraordinary success. Lorin Hollander, a virtuoso completely in tune with his generation, is the son of an orchestra-musician father who plays in the TV ensemble backing Perry Como, who in turn tendered Lorin a glamorous debut before many millions. Peter Serkin, now that we've mentioned sons, owes at least some of his career to Papa Rudolf's prestige. And André Watts, suddenly thrust into mass attention via Bernstein's televised youth concerts, is also one of those blessed by "the laying on of hands." A conductor or some other established luminary is often able to open doors for a favored protégé.

Needless to say, not one of these people, any more than the prizewinners, would have had the shadow of a chance without his own individual gifts and the training to match them. We publicity-minded and charisma-conscious Americans can be quite naive about this, generously labeling anybody who's played at a club musicale a "concert pianist," and so easily assuming that a hopeful who's won a little local and regional recognition is a sure thing for the Big Thing. To reduce this generalization to an absurd minimum, I have in front of me a clipping from a music publication, which makes rather sad reading. Under the headline, "Meteoric Rise of Young Pianist," it relates that "The pretty and smiling young artist of 16, ——, the pupil of Mrs. ——, Midwest City, USA, continues her rise to fame and fortune with the achievements of her high level of virtuosity on the piano...."

After reading of this young lady's success in the National Piano Playing Auditions, we go on to discover that she has dazzled the judges successively at the Piano Achievement Contest, at the State Music Teachers Association Competition, and at the Women's Association Contest of her Home Town Symphony Orchestra. The heady climax is that, thanks to the last-named organization, our young friend is to have "a full four-year scholarship at a metropolitan school of music."

An accomplishment, certainly, at this early stage

of training. From the vantage point of a very small town, one might well see a "meteoric rise." But the "fame and fortune" bit—and in a professional magazine no less—is as sweetly unrealistic as a romantic Hollywood fadeout of the 1930s. In one sense, it's a hangover, just one more symptom of a competition-happy environment.

Careers *can* be won without major prizes, but unfortunately, the opposite is also true: major prizes can be won without leading to careers or anything much in the way of fame or fortune. And once begun, careers can droop and fade just as easily with a prize built into them as without.

Some musicians even make a kind of career, for as long as they can, of contests themselves. There are also examples—Cliburn among them—of artists going for another run at a contest if their careers lose momentum and before they become overage. In one case, a violinist won a Leventritt during the mid-1940s, stamping him as ready "for an immediate career as a concert artist"; and then, to give his career a transfusion twelve years later, he entered the Naumburg Foundation contest only to emerge second to an orchestral violinist.

As prizes proliferate, the more readily their captors' names evaporate. It's not surprising that we Americans don't remember all the post-Cliburn winners in Moscow. But what about those in the heart of Texas, at the international contest carrying the Cliburn name? There have been three Cliburn competitions as of this writing, each with a top prize of $10,000, an RCA Victor recording contract, plus concerto and recital appearances under the management of S. Hurok. If you happen to know that the first prize went to American Ralph Votapek in 1962, to the Rumanian Radu Lupu in 1966, and to the Brazilian Cristina Ortiz in 1969, you are better informed than most musicians. Just try a quiz on the second prize winners!

Even so, successful competitors have at least picked up a smattering of prestige and some good engagements along with their prize money. And when you look over the musical names that are well known, from the middle and younger generations of concert artists, you're likely to see prizes somewhere in the background. Among Leventritt winners alone are not only Cliburn and Frager but John Browning, Sydney Foster, Gary Graffman, and Eugene Istomin. John Ogdon is another successful, non-Russian Moscow prizewinner. And several of the Russian victors have come under the aegis of Hurok; pianists Vladimir Ashkenazy, Alexander Slobodyanik, and Grigory Sokolov are among the new Soviet elite to be taken under his wing. Hurok likes successful Americans, too. When the young pianist Misha Dichter came home from placing second to the still younger Sokolov in the 1966 Tchaikovsky, he had made such an impression on Russian audiences that both Hurok and RCA Victor, who had been lukewarm when approached before, were on hand with contracts.

There's little doubt that, for all its uncertainties and mirages, the major competition has been behaving very much like a permanent fixture. And whether or not it "works" for all the right people, it can still be distinctly useful—even for the also-rans, if they can stay in the running. Many young Americans have become what I call, perhaps too harshly, "chronic contestants," not only in hopes of the prize money and the added engagements, but also because there is virtually no other opportunity for them to appear, to develop poise before audiences, to learn to project themselves and to mature their art—all so vitally necessary to a polished performer and personality.

The steady availability of precisely such experiences is what affords young Soviet aspirants so great an advantage in contests. Once a talent emerges, it is specifically singled out and trained for artistic competition in the way that youngsters of other nations are primed for athletic competitions. These young Soviet musicians have no finer training than ours; but they are told, for example, that in two years or three years they are to be scheduled, if they

99

merit it, to enter the Brussels Competition, or the Leventritt Competition, or the Cliburn Competition. No detours. No distractions. They are guided and directed in working up the specified repertories. When these works are ready for the public, the public hears them at perhaps twenty-five recitals and twenty appearances with orchestras around Russia. There is no scrounging around by the musicians, no begging for chances or for money.

The next year they are given more and more important appearances. Eventually, they walk into a competition with complete conviction, with confidence born of experience. Each elimination round is merely another concert for them, one more of the many that they have been playing before any number of previous audiences. No wonder they do well.

In contrast, our young artists are struggling to get enough time to practice after teaching long hours for small fees. There's too little time for proper practice or study, too little money to provide more than a minimal subsistence, even if the candidates are lucky enough to be among the comparatively few who are aided financially by our State Department, the Institute of International Education, the Martha Baird Rockefeller Foundation, or similar organizations.

Before this partial help became available, our

representation in contests was completely hit-or-miss. There was the competition year in Brussels, for example, when the official United States entry was a girl who just happened to be in town and decided it would be fun to enter. Today the IIE sends abroad about thirty contestants a year, screened by its own sixty-man committee. Adrian Larkin, who manages this program, has a special affection for the competitions at Geneva and Munich, these being among the few that admit performers on virtually any instrument.

In this way, then, a certain number of Americans who are not under management and therefore have few prospects of recitals can pick up valuable experience, even at times with orchestra. Few people realize the vast competition and concert experience that Van Cliburn had before he went to Russia. Six years earlier, he had won the Chopin Competition in New York. Two years after that, his extraordinary performances at the Leventritt Competition won not only first place but a managerial contract that kept Cliburn busy for two years playing recital and orchestral dates up and down the land to enormous critical acclaim. And even though his career then approached a dead end, he had already been equipped to ride his success at Moscow further than he ever could have otherwise.

In art, few worthwhile things are accidental. Toscanini used to say, "Nothing happens in performance that hasn't happened in rehearsal, except the bad things!" And Malcolm Frager told me he looked on his contest experiences as an exam, an opportunity to show how well he'd studied. If that is so, I suppose the dangers and inequities of a contest are those inherent in any crucially competitive and selective exam.

Misha Dichter is convinced that there is a "competition type," who "plays quickly, cleanly, and without offending anyone." In his opinion, Artur Schnabel, perhaps the greatest Beethoven interpreter of this century, wouldn't have had a chance. Neither, in all probability, would Rudolf Serkin.

Seymour Lipkin, a superbly gifted pianist who won the arduous and now-defunct Rachmaninoff Award in 1948 but who has been rerouted by conductorial gifts and opportunities (no less than the "laying on of hands" by the late George Szell in Cleveland), is convinced that "competitions are basically artificial in that the performer is not giving something to the public. He is simply trying to demonstrate his prowess." Lipkin sees the underlying problem in an American public which "is being systematically trained not to decide for itself. We are supposed to trust the advertisements and not our individual judgment." He has touched on a serious weakness, which brings to mind the apron strings that tie theatergoers to opinions in newspapers or on television, and prevent them from developing and using their own criteria.

This hit-or-flop syndrome of ours sometimes makes for a totally illogical discrepancy between the recognition accorded a winner and that given a runner-up. For example, while Cliburn after his 1958 win was escorted up Broadway with ticker tape and bands, Joyce Flissler, a prizewinner in the violin competition, returned to New York completely unsung and unstrung. There were no reporters, no cameras to greet the valiant young woman who had survived all the preliminaries into the finals, and had then finished eighth among violinists *from all over the world*. Nor has her prize since accounted for a single additional American engagement or dollar of income. In sharp contrast, all of the finalists in Russia were honored, not only the winners, and were almost equally esteemed as artists. They were immediately booked for tours to Kiev, Riga, Odessa, etc., and Miss Flissler was sent to perform in Leningrad, in itself a signal honor. But no one back home said "well done" except personal friends and secure colleagues.

The New York debut recital can of course be just as cruel and lonely in its own way. Harold Schonberg, the *New York Times* critic, remembers an occasion years ago in Carnegie Recital Hall when

103

the audience consisted of one listener and two critics—the pianist having booked the hall on his own, without a manager and without any publicity. Halfway through the program the performer broke down and cried. The critics felt like joining him. And the leverage of even well-attended debuts hasn't improved since then.

Occasionally somebody comes up with a new idea. Leon Fleisher, the first American to win a major European competition (first prize in the Queen Elisabeth of Belgium contest), suggested that managements might open a special department using a panel of their artists who happen to be within reach. The panel would listen to young hopefuls who want to audition and the manager would take the panel's recommendations. Maybe it would work. Most of the managers I know, however, place almost inviolable trust in their own judgment—even though this may be prompted by the decisions of contest judges.

On the other hand, managers can vary distinctly in their opinions and attitudes, as the next chapter discloses.

Another suggestion regarding contests was made by pianist Abbey Simon, winner of the Naumburg award in 1940, to Shirley Fleming of *Musical America*. He proposes that each country limit itself to a national competition every four or five years, sending its winners on to a single big international contest. This, he feels, "would give an artist a chance to mature." But just think what it would demand from judges in responsibility and crystal-gazing to pick a world champion for the coming five years!

Though a competition may put one or more of its contestants into orbit, it will not, as we have seen, keep them there indefinitely. In the long pull of a career it's up to the individual's own musician-ship, virtuosity, and flair or charisma—or whatever you want to call that elusive third element. Even Cliburn's unique break would have petered out long ago if he weren't both the superior pianist and the outgoing, communicative personality that he is—all of which, of course, helped make the break possible in the first place.

Pointing out that more than one competition winner in recent history has subsided from the con-test stage back into the orchestra pit or the music faculty of a sequestered midwestern college, mana-ger Herbert Barrett feels that the only certainty to expect from a competition "is that the winner will have a better opportunity to prove that he has what it takes." And pianist Malcolm Frager, estimating the effect of his double take of the Leventritt and the Queen Elisabeth, mentioned that each had been helpful on its own side of the Atlantic in facilitating engagements apart from those "built in" for successful competitors.

"But, should I return," he added emphatically, "then that's *me*."

Even the Russian contestants, one notices, have their ups and downs. The twenty-nine-year-old Slobodyanik entered the Warsaw Competition at the age of sixteen and placed seventh—not surprising considering his youth. But the experience hit him hard. He stopped practicing and in due course was expelled from the Moscow Conservatory. Later after more sober reflection, he reapplied successfully and at twenty-four placed a fourth in the 1966 Tchaikovsky contest. Thereupon, he played quite a bit around the USSR but nothing much happened.

In 1969 he came to New York. Hurok heard him and offered him a contract without stopping to inquire whether he had come first, middle, or last in the competitions. Nobody else seemed to care either. Obviously, each career is unique. Without the need to compete again, Slobodyanik began to get the best dates—and the worst reviews. For example, he was booked for a glamourous date usually reserved for established artists with prestige plus box office power—the opening night of the New York Philharmonic. As first soloist of the 1970–71 season, playing the Rachmaninoff *Third Concerto* under Bernstein's baton, he elicited from the *Times* critic Schonberg a lethal review ending with the comment "Poor Rachmaninoff!"

The big competition news of 1969–70 was the capture of the Cliburn Competition's first prize by nineteen-year-old Brazilian beauty, pianist Cristina Ortiz, and the New York appearances of four male pianists from four different corners of the world, all in their twenties, all victors in prestigious competitions.

First came the Israeli Joseph Kalichstein. Following his conquest of the twenty-sixth Leventritt Award, he appeared with the Cleveland Symphony under Szell in the Beethoven *Fourth Concerto*, playing with an impressive command of his instrument and the music which stamped him instantly as a significant talent.

The most sensational event was the debut recital of Minoru Nojima, the Japanese winner of the Cliburn Competition's second prize. Taking on the toughest of all tests, a Carnegie Hall solo program of immense scope and difficulty, he won an ovation from a full house teeming with distinguished musicians and received a unanimous set of rave reviews that the town had not read of any pianist since the debut of Horowitz four decades before.

Another kind of victory was announced in two-column news flashes from Warsaw, Poland, where the American Garrick Ohlsson had captured the

Chopin International Piano Prize. The six-foot four-inch young man, only twenty-two years old, had won two international prizes within the previous four years, the Busoni and the Montreal, without making much of a mark on the concert platform. Perhaps in remembrance of the classic Cliburn case, Ohlsson decided on another try. As the first American ever to win the Polish competition, his victory stimulated considerably more publicity than others did, and Eugene Ormandy invited Ohlsson to appear with the Philadelphia Orchestra in New York immediately upon his return.

His soloist vehicle was the Chopin *E Minor Concerto* with which he had conquered a field of eighty pianists. Hearing Mr. Ohlsson for the first time, I could only hope and conclude that the jury's decision was based on his playing of other works, for surely this concerto's essential style and sentiments seemed quite alien to this young pianist, and one must wait before formulating a comprehensive opinion on his technical and musical qualities. Meanwhile, the performance reminded me of another by Maurizio Pollini, who a decade before had won the same prize for the same concerto and displayed the same unawareness of what this beautiful work should evoke.

Equally disappointing was the appearance of

Vladimir Krainev, who tied with pianist John Lill of England for the first Tchaikovsky prize in Moscow. As soloist with the Washington Symphony in the great Russian's "sure-fire" *Concerto in B-flat Minor*, the young Soviet demonstrated that even it can misfire when not handled by a first-class virtuoso and a sensitive musician. From first to last, Mr. Krainev sounded thoroughly uncomprehending and uncomfortable. A follow-up recital led critics to suggest that the time had come for Krainev to unlearn many of the things he had been taught; to take a break and really start studying.

I speak of these matters with deep concern and apprehension, having judged many competitions for many years. During the past ten years it has been painful to observe the gradual spiral downward of performance standards. I have heard a large number of competition contestants of numerous nationalities in contests, classes, and concerts. Out of perhaps some three hundred pianists, violinists, and cellists ranging widely in pedagogical advantages and in age from fifteen to thirty, surprisingly few emerged who by reasonably professional standards could be said to have more than a modest measure of talent and competence. I have just checked my carefully notated reactions and can count only thirty-one competitors in all that time who impressed me as having "a splendid equip-

ment," or "a genuine gift, well on its way to fulfillment," or "real individuality and command."
Only nine struck me as "superior, and in every
way."

Almost all the others were without any real distinction, and the saddest were the scholarship-hold-
ing students from eminent universities whose
dossiers read "D. Mus. in progress," for invariably
they turned out to be the most limited, the most
handicapped.

I cannot explain it, but it did reveal to me the
basis of a famous remark by the late Leopold Godowsky, whose acidulous humor was hardly less
famed than his art. During a final illness, the celebrated composer-pianist was told that a scheduled
operation was extremely serious. "And," the doctor
added, "I must perform my professional duty to
advise you, dear Leopold, that if you have any final
wishes, you should make them known."

"My dear friend," said Godowsky, whose wit
never deserted him, not even at this dreadful moment, "I have but one final wish. Please don't let
any Doctor of Music get near me!"

Again I must apologize for this brief digression,
but these matters inevitably arise in connection
with contestants who hope that competitions will
somehow be their open sesame to the professional
world. Not one among the hundreds I have heard

has a ghost of a chance. As I listen to them I keep wondering, what are they going to do, these "Doctors of Music"? Where are they headed? If this degree-mill continues grinding at its usual pace, it will simply turn out ever more "professors" who are merely able to teach others to teach still others still less. Contests are not for them. That game is to the swift; that battle to the strong, and the strongly equipped.

Finally, no discussion of contests can exclude the vast and venerable Young Artist Auditions held biennially by the National Federation of Music Clubs. Geared toward gifted young pianists, violinists, and singers, male and female, the nationwide competitions offer cash prizes, scholarships, orchestral and solo appearances to the successful candidate.

As in other competitions, the highest standards are eagerly sought, but necessarily depend upon the quality of entrants and judges. But at all times and for over half a century, the federation's policies and practices have been thoroughly realistic, its prizes unpretentious, its philosophy entirely professional.

This immense organization has discovered hundreds of talents and has provided unusually constructive opportunities often leading to solid fulfillment. Instead of the hoopla of the giant competitions that too often catapult contestants to heights they cannot sustain, the federation offers an unassuming program that encourages and nurtures the precious material of talent. It's still part of the only game in town, but the odds are more favorable to all but the one-in-a-million genius who is not subject to the averages.

7

The Concert Manager: Endangered Species

*A*s we have seen, competitions—provided a contestant wins, places, or shows—may serve to light the obscurity that usually surrounds the musician at the early stages of a career. And if a New York recital award is offered, the sizable financial burden of such an appearance may be happily avoided.

But the big question of management, unless this too is automatically resolved by a contest victory, arises from the moment that a graduate emerges from the protective environment of the conservatory or college and contemplates a solo career.

There will be no musical personnel men swarming over campus to correspond to those eager representatives of IBM, General Electric, and Dupont with their special enticements for special students. In music, it's the other way around. The gifted and ambitious graduate must use every means of enticing the interest of managers who are too busy finding engagements for musicians already under contract even to think of adding anyone new and unproven to their roster of responsibilities. A hard fact, perhaps, but one that applies to all but a handful of artists.

Incidentally, the great majority of this handful will be men, and not because there are fewer fine artists on the distaff side. It is simply that most local booking committees are mainly staffed by and invariably administered by women. Most of the seats in concert halls are occupied by women, not to mention the seats next to them that are occupied *because* of women. As the ad used to remind us, never underestimate their power—or their preference.

All buyers and sellers of artists are well aware of such basic facts, as one can see from the artists on the rosters of the three primary kinds of managements.

114

First, there are the artist managers and representatives, now led in size and quantity of business by the mammoth Columbia Artists Management, Inc., and its subsidiary, Community Concerts, which provides organizational, promotional, and booking service to over eight hundred communities throughout the United States and Canada. They and other artist managements, such as the Herbert Barrett and Ann Colbert offices, are organized into the International Association of Concert and Festival Managers. Then there is the one and only Sol Hurok, the Svengali of superstars and spectacles.

The second category is that of concert managers, who book performers into their local halls in towns and cities across the country, and who most often double as lawyers or druggists or in some other profession or business.

The third category might be called that of administrators, including salaried state and community arts council managers. It also includes unsalaried concert series administrators on campus, who are organized as the Association of College and University Concert Managers (ACUCM). These university people are different from managers in that they buy rather than sell artists, and from every available source, and in this they are essentially noncommercial in orientation.

This chapter deals mainly with the artist managers, since it is through them that the professional performer comes to public attention. And again we must stress that the artist manager, far from seeking out new names for a list he may already consider overlong, tends to protect himself from possible inundation by being "hard to get." Success in an important contest will be more likely than any other factor to open his office door—a crack, anyway.

But let us be optimistic and assume that some manager has become interested enough to add a new artist's name to his list. Let us further assume that he is booking his client across the country wherever he can; that he is formulating long-range career plans that will help the artist; and that the artist for his part is cooperating intelligently and learning all he can from the manager's suggestions. A good start, but far from stardom.

The primary problem, throughout the various segments of "the industry," is inadequate communication between most artists, managers, and buyers. For instance, it wasn't until manager Harold Shaw (during his association with Hurok Attractions) attended a Johnson Foundation conference at Racine, Wisconsin, on the problems of the professional performing arts on campus in May, 1968, that he learned of two country-wide surveys made in 1965 and 1967 by the ACUCM to discover the cultural profile and character of its member institutions. He found himself "appalled" at the "terrible communications gap," and urged closer ties among all who are concerned with the mechanics of presenting concerts.

Later in the same conference, Mr. Shaw urged both the university people and his fellow artist managers, all of whom deplored the current state of the business, to get over the "big guns attitude": in other words, to be willing to try lesser-known performers in smaller halls. "We need the audience of 150," he said. "We've got to get back and accept the fact that concern and curiosity about newcomers is a specific interest, a minority taste; and if we treat it as such, we will find the young artists to help develop."

Later, during a rash of managerial alterations and alliances, Mr. Shaw set himself up in his own independent management, which may enable him to implement his ideas. Another independent declaration came from William Judd, a top executive of the daddy of 'em all, Columbia. Why, after a thirty-year association, did he take this surprising step, especially at this uncertain time? "Because," was his answer, "I want to return to the personalized guidance of artists' careers, which only an independent manager can provide." Shaw and Judd

117

should inspire young artists of quality to genuine optimism.

The next significant managerial announcement came from a huge organization, Transcontinental Investing Corporation, which in the fall of 1969 acquired the Hurok empire. Two years later TIC sold its interests to General Electric. The acquisition indicates pointedly the technological trend of musical entertainment.

One of the Racine conferees was managerial executive Sheldon Gold, who reminded me that "several years ago the study made by Baumol and Bowen for the Twentieth Century Fund on the economic problems common to the performing arts indicated that approximately 3 per cent of our population buys one ticket per year for one so-called cultural event in the United States. That's a tragic figure to start with, in view of the highly advertised 'cultural explosion'—and the figure had not grown anywhere near the population increase itself."

Mr. Gold is also convinced of the need for "some extraordinary gimmick to produce a charisma and to create a public excitement," without which even the mature, established artist may be in trouble. This further explains the almost desperate popularity of contests among young artists and managers.

Herbert Barrett, who created and heads perhaps the largest independent management, is more prone to observe, at this critical moment, than to state conclusions. He finds the Baroque revival "encouraging and compensating somewhat for the undeniable falling off otherwise in soloistic bookings. Especially it has helped harpsichordists and classical guitarists, with a boost also for some violinists." (Barrett did not mention the hit recordings of Yehudi Menuhin with Ravi Shankar, which reflected the short-lived hysteria over Indian culture.)

Mr. Barrett also commented, somewhat wryly, on the curious fact that though there seems to be a genuine renaissance in chamber music—"Think of that beautiful Alice Tully Hall at Lincoln Center, built entirely for chamber music!"—the low-fee tradition persists as in the old days. "One could book Serkin as a soloist for $1,500; but when he played with his violinist father-in-law, Adolf Busch, all I ever got for them both together was $1,000, family rates!" he said.

"But each day a more serious problem arises, in dealing with group performances," said Barrett. "We not only face constant escalation of union rates, but the necessity of dealing with five, six, and even more unions to mount one non-solo event. And there's no stopping it, for that's what unions are for, that's their business." The answer?

119

"Subsidy, any and all kinds. Otherwise, we're sunk," Barrett said. "Look at Austria, little Austria. Geographically a dot compared to our country, with a smaller population than Manhattan. But last year its government spent three times what ours did on music."

In this connection, the entire program of federal aid to the arts has since been well served by the appointment of Nancy Hanks, a former executive of the Rockefeller Brothers Fund, as chairman of the National Council of the Arts. She has made staunch efforts not only to stimulate financial assistance to the arts but also to promote higher standards within the cultural activities of the country.

High cultural standards have also characterized the long-held ideals and practices of the most powerful of concert managers, Sol Hurok. This P. T. Barnum of the musical world remains something of a law unto himself, the one manager whom associates and colleagues unanimously insist on calling "impresario," with all the grandiose connotations of that title. "Sol," as he is known affectionately by the entire professional world, loves and respects his stars, but he also watches over their audiences the way a croupier studies roulette players.

Characteristic is his classic answer to the question, "What is it that makes one artist a furor and another a fiasco, though both may be equally great?"

"Very simple," answers Sol, loftily. "When people don't want to come, nothing will stop them!"

Everyone knows Sol as the prime promoter of the most glamorous soloists and groups in the world. Throughout his career, however, he has been persuaded to lend his genius to the development of some young talents, including the winners of various prestigious competitions. Since very few of them have made the grade and a surprising number have simply dropped into limbo, I thought it more tactful to question Martin Feinstein, the Hurok publicity director who was once described by his boss, in answer to a query from Mme. André Malraux, as "*my* cultural minister."

"It's an extraordinary thing," Feinstein told me, "how many people are under the impression that all any artist has to do is to get into Hurok's stable to become a champ. That isn't so at all, as more than a few artists have discovered; they had to bite the bitter dust to learn that music is not essentially a democratic art. No matter how liberally artists are exposed, it's no guarantee of popularity.

"Every buyer knows, of course, that a big management can deliver a great attraction. The implication is always present: 'Perhaps we may be able to get you Rubinstein or the Bolshoi Ballet, and we hope that you will also take one of our younger people. . . .' But even that is no open road to success, for big managements as well as small managements are in the same position of having to build careers; and unless something fantastic happens—something like the Cliburn bombshell—this may take a matter of years. If it ever happens."

Fortunately, there have been many idealistic, nonprofit efforts made over the years to aid inexperienced artists. Most have foundered on practical problems of competition and money, but a few survive and remain among the most important sources of encouragement and support for our young talent.

The most venerable of the nonprofit managements is the National Music League, founded in 1927. The league sets an age limit of thirty-two on the applicants it auditions; books those it accepts for not more than five years in fully professional situations; and takes the usual commissions. However, since the fees its young artists command are usually nominal and the time it gives to individual planning and guidance is large, there is a built-in operating deficit that must be met through outside help.

Alfred Rossin, the league's experienced director,

sees a great need for the educational side of his work. "Young artists," he says, "tend to be the most innocent souls alive. They are graduated from the finest conservatories or universities, but most of them don't know how to dress for the platform, don't know how to walk or bow gracefully, and evidently never gave a thought to the business or public-relations aspects of a musical career."

Among the brightest luminaries whom Mr. Rossin has "graduated" over the years into commercial management are vocalists Rise Stevens and Shirley Verrett and pianist Philippe Entremont, who made his debut under league management at the age of sixteen.

When I asked Mr. Rossin how many young artists taken up by nonprofit groups have found a reasonably successful life in music, his estimate was between 50 and 60 per cent, most of whom have also gone into teaching. He is pleased at the developing artist-in-residence and affiliate artist opportunities, but observes that the more money the universities have to spend, the more they gravitate toward the glamour of the Big Name.

Considerably more optimistic is young Susan Popkin Wadsworth, who about a decade ago, while still in her teens, presented a series of concerts in a Greenwich Village restaurant. Today her Young

Concert Artists offers an annual series in New York and others in Boston, Pittsburgh, Cincinnati, and Louisville.

Mrs. Wadsworth, like the league, books young artists (they must be between eighteen and twenty-eight years old) wherever else they can be sold, and though she puts no limit on their terms of association, she has lost some protégés rather quickly. Gaily and in her characteristically unselfish way, she relates how two of her artists—pianist Misha Dichter, after placing second in the 1966 Tchaikovsky contest, and violinist Pinchas Zukerman, after capturing the 1968 Leventritt Award—were both swept up by the indefatigable Sol Hurok.

As a nonprofit management, Mrs. Wadsworth's services are free. There is but a token commission on booked-and-paid-for-by-others dates. For the 1970–71 season, she booked over one hundred engagements for eighteen young artists who are earning between $400 and $500 per concert.

When I inquired about others she had picked (Mrs. Wadsworth personally selects about two dozen of the best out of perhaps two hundred applicants and then enlists a highly qualified jury for her finals), she said, "A gratifying number of them are doing very well—and many of them, like Misha and Pinchas, have already acquired major performing careers under commercial managements."

Another nonprofit management, Concert Artists Guild, was created and directed by Mrs. Blanche Wise, who later affiliated it with New York University and Town Hall. It has sponsored solo recitals each season without fee or commission since 1951, and also has conducted a number of "Debut-Award Concerts" which offer two young soloists the opportunity of jointly making their first New York public appearances. Among those the organization has selected are vocalists Evelyn Lear and George Shirley.

Mrs. Wise, no longer actively associated with the organization, expressed some doubts as to the ultimate usefulness of competitions for any prizes but concert dates.

"Actually, I've been shocked," she said, "to read some of the dossiers of our applicants, to see how many contests they've entered and emerged from as runners-up, or fifth, or nowhere. What I can't figure out is when they had the time to study, to practice."

"Perhaps they haven't," I suggested, "and despairing of winning first prizes at contests, they land at your place seeking management."

"That's fine with me," she answered, "because

125

the most valuable thing we can do is exactly to give youngsters a chance to be heard and evaluated, by judges, by critics, and by others. The whole process and preparation drives them to study hard. But then, as we work along with them for at least three years trying to book them as advantageously as we can, we get discouraged again, because it still can be a terribly rough ride even for contest winners. Very few survive intact, let alone triumphantly. And just try to get institutions to help youngsters. How many give a damn?"

Well, exactly two, so far as I know: the Martha Baird Rockefeller Fund, with a specific interest in young performing artists, and the Institute of International Education, dedicated to aiding young artists to participate in contests abroad, as it did Van Cliburn when it paid for his Moscow trip.

Fortunately for a few career-seeking soloists, some of the smaller managements are better geared to the care and feeding of the neophyte than are the big operators: that of Ann Summers, for example. Another is the office of Norman Seaman, who for years has been making possible economy-priced, informal debuts at Town Hall and who, through his Concert Club, distributes free and marked-down tickets to over one hundred New York concerts a season, bringing in young people from Harlem and elsewhere to what may be their first concerts anywhere. This service is dependent upon the cooperation of other managements desirous of filling halls for their lesser-known artists.

What the buyers and sellers, and all the other people in this sphere ultimately care most about, of course, is not the arts administrator, not the local concert management, not even the artist himself, but the audiences, without which none of the rest could exist. They are aided and abetted in this concern by a splendid nonprofit organization called Young Audiences, which fits available musicians—and especially ensembles—into school schedules so that they can not only play for the children and talk to them about the music, but above all can get the children themselves talking. During a recent season, this twenty-year-old organization, under the direction of Carol Morse, gave almost twelve thousand concerts using about nine hundred musicians. It is active in thirty-one states and has so far established forty Young Audience chapters in schools.

To round off this survey, I have culled from prominent managements some authoritative opinions on some of the basic questions.

Feinstein: "The musical field, like all other entertainment fields, is dominated by the star-performer psychology. It has virtues and vices. Many young artists who play superbly well do not gain a hearing because the dollar-conscious ticket-buyer insists that he 'get the best'—i.e. the star (who may not necessarily be the best). Sad to say, inflation is probably the biggest factor in the arts today. Our young people have trouble getting hearings, not because of cultural centers or their lack, but because the costs of presentation, advertising, etc. are identical for the young artist as they are for the star—in fact, they may be even more onerous. Unfortunately, our old-time managers who used to carry the artists on subscription series dominated by stars have largely died out because of the economics of the business. We also have the phenomenon today of rising costs prohibiting many organizations from traveling to smaller cities. For example, it is impossible for big companies like the Bolshoi Opera or the Royal Ballet to visit any but the largest cities. The road is not dying; it is dead." Early in 1972 Mr. Feinstein acted on these convictions by terminating his twenty-five-year association with Hurok to become executive director of performing arts at the Kennedy Center in Washington, D.C.

Thea Dispeker: "Commercial audiences may be growing smaller. But the extent of all-round listening, of small-time concert-going, is rising all over the country. It's *got* to, with the quality of the musicians we've been developing here."

Rossin: "Despite the specious ferment known as the 'cultural explosion,' art in our country always has taken second place, and I think it's growing steadily worse. We are not building audiences. Cultural centers are a disastrous development for the young performer. Large and expensive buildings have to attract lots of people, and you can only do that with a few great names or celebrated groups of some sort. Frankly, I think that if this keeps up, the concert as we know it, except for a handful of stars, may soon be nonexistent."

Gold: "Except for the compelling personality there is no interest, no money, no real future. Don't forget that two factors loom most significantly—the age-old personality cult and the brand-new phenomenon of the sovereignty of youth in every aspect of life and art."

Ann Colbert: "There has been no decline in bookings for our finest artists and chamber groups. The American concert public has become so sophisticated, so selective, that it demands the highest artistic standards. No longer is it possible for mediocre or routine performers to survive in the fiercely super-competitive market of this country."

129

At the end of 1970, two managerial conferences in New York brought the leading booking groups and personalities together, as the International Association of Concert and Festival Managers conclave was immediately followed by that of the Association of College and University Managers.

The prevailing mood of numerous speeches and discussions was reflected by the stark title of the IACFM convention, "Survival—Is There a Future for the Arts?"

The organization's president, Gail W. Rector, considers the current scene "an enormous challenge, which all of us must meet by recognizing and overcoming the undeniable difficulties within the classical concert field. There is new awareness and new blood within our industry, and now there is a new determination to face facts and to welcome innovations that appear timely and promising. This is not only within our power, but it is also our basic responsibility. If we won't assume it, who will?"

As a panelist, Harold Shaw said, "We must admit that the youngsters' criticisms of college concert managers are not all unfounded. Many of us have *not* assumed our responsibilities properly. The kids want to share in a trust previously given to us and which we obviously administered in too relaxed a manner, or perhaps even poorly at times.

The time is not only ripe, but running out for us to do whatever we can to revitalize every aspect of musical art and business."

These are some of the points of view to which the young performer, if he finds and opens the door to management, will entrust his career. In general, the more pessimistic among these people seem to be looking at the business statistics, while the others, so far as possible, aren't. It may be that the latter are unrealistic and therefore misleading to the career-minded musician.

Yet anyone who feels that music is going down to ruin may be related distantly to certain aerodynamic experts who once concluded that the hummingbird, on the basis of wingspread and other measurable factors, cannot fly.

But the hummingbird, to our great encouragement, goes on flying anyway.

8

The Amateur and the Astronaut

*I*f this book were a "how to" manual for the hopeful young musician, we would now be ready to tidy up a few stray admonitions, pat the young hopeful on the head, and send him off to a promising career. But it could not have been such a manual or anything like it, not an honest one and not today, at any rate. Navigation is impossible to teach in shallow waters and in a channel that keeps shifting.

To extend this metaphor and to sum up some

previous observations, we note floundering support for traditional performances, while the deadly serious avant garde continues to spin in its tiny eddies. Simultaneously, rock is still running at flood tide with youth the world over. Minor flirtations with jazz and Baroque and, more recently, wanton plunges into computerized constructions, and the maelstrom of mixed media complete the scene.

And now what? Nobody pretends to know. Contemplating the future of music in all its aspects leads to knotty questions too hard to untie. Will this or that style or idiom continue to shine with a lovely, steady light or gutter and die out? The old, comfortable popular-classical polarizations are leveling off, most notably in the occasional striving of pop music toward expressions of symphonic and operatic intent and dimension.

Meanwhile, there is a somber accompaniment to the lip-service paid in high places to the importance of the arts in American life. Let's start to grow up and take as hard a look at our esthetic status as we have been forced to take at our economic and ecological condition. The low priority of the arts and higher education in the United States vis-à-vis rocketing scientific and military expenditures is matched only by the public apathy over the life-and-death struggles of our cultural institutions.

133

The major responsibility rests clearly upon the federal government, since the states and the municipalities are already swamped by their own financial misfortunes, and the great foundations are the newest tax targets. And for what? The overwhelming burden of unimaginable sums of money to support a tragic war. Amid the groping for international peace, amid our urban and environmental catastrophes, amid our social and educational crises, the chief sources of possible survival for our society—knowledge, culture, and reason— are being systematically starved. Can anyone in his right mind think that the Pentagon's mammoth budget offers our society a better chance of developing, of attaining a higher quality of living than if a fraction of its allocations were reallocated for the youth of our country, for our academic and cultural institutions?

Unless we drastically shift our priorities, how can we develop the disciplined and far-sighted leaders so desperately needed? Never in our history has it been so important for us to demonstrate our own priorities as individuals, what we hold most important, less important, least important. Precisely this—our ideas of how life should be lived—is the central issue being articulated and exemplified on our embattled campuses today.

The greatness of our country is due immeasur-

THE AMATEUR AND THE ASTRONAUT

ably to a large number of idealistic leaders, who arose in every field of endeavor—even in the military!

Not long ago I discovered that Neil Armstrong, the first man on the moon, is not only a space hero for our time, not only a reader of the Bible, but also a musician who can get around a bit on the piano and who plays a fairly mean baritone horn. The *way* I found it out tends to confirm our indifference to the arts, since the information came not through any big-circulation news medium but in an article published in a trade journal and originated as a promotion piece by the manufacturers of Mr. Armstrong's horn! Even so, the news was somehow exhilarating—including word from the astronaut's mother that whenever he came home from a mission he gave his first attention to the piano. "Only after he had played three or four things, was he ready to sit down and tell us what he had been doing."

That's the kind of priority any musician will recognize. "Humanity's most daring adventurer," he'll think to himself, "the man whose 'small step' became 'a giant leap for mankind,' why, he's one of *us!*" Perhaps a realistic antidote for the current professional gloom lies in a seemingly obscure and isolated fact: that Neil Armstrong's love for music was instilled in him as a small-town midwestern kid, at about the same time he determined to fly. By whom? By his mother. And who had lit the spark in her? A piano teacher who belonged to a widespread, deeply rooted organization so woven into the fabric of our life that most of us hardly notice it. Yet, this book would be incomplete in its service if it failed to take note of the National Guild of Piano Teachers and of its founder and president emeritus, Irl Allison.

To do some scene-setting at this point requires a look backward to the turn-of-the-century state of small-town cultural innocence summed up by the Stage Manager in Thornton Wilder's play *Our Town*. In answer to a superior question about its artistic life, he says: "Well . . . there's some girls that play the piano over at High School Commencement: but they ain't happy about it. . . . No, ma'am, there isn't much culture . . .—Robinson Crusoe and the Bible; and Handel's Largo, we all know *that*; and Whistler's Mother—those are just about as far as we go."

Then there's a story about Paderewski, from a few years after the time Wilder is describing, when the celebrated pianist's touring took him to a small western town. Finding himself with some free time before his concert, he strolled about. As he passed a house that displayed a large shingle reading "Debena Smith—Teacher of Piano," he heard the

strains of his famous *Minuet*. Appalled by the plethora of mistakes and distortions, Paderewski
bounded up the steps and rang the doorbell.

The sounds ceased and a lady opened the door.
One glance into the empty room told Paderewski
that it was no inept pupil but the teacher herself who
had been murdering his music. When Miss Smith
recognized the familiar face of the master, she
blushed with embarrassment. With old-world
courtliness, Paderewski murmured that he was flat-
tered to hear his composition and had intruded
upon her only to offer a few suggestions that might
contribute to the effectiveness of her interpretation. Tactfully, he pointed out the most flagrant
errors; then quickly bowed himself out and fled.

Two years later Paderewski played again in the
same town and as his taxi passed the unforgettable
house, he saw that a much larger shingle had replaced the earlier one. The new sign proclaimed:
"Debena Smith—Teacher of Piano—Pupil of Paderewski."

This has never been a funny story to me. It
speaks too poignantly of those thousands of cheated
children, victims of ignorant lesson sellers who dare
to call themselves teachers. They are less plentiful
now, for which we owe many thanks to Irl Allison.
But suppose, in those days, a fortunate youngster
far from the hub *did* find good teaching. If he

137

was unusually gifted, there might arise some incentives for him after a while in some unprestigious regional or national contests. If not, and even if he began his study with strong interest in music itself, he could soon feel the lack of stimulation, study goals, and recognition within his attainable range. Dr. Allison was the man who found an answer for this built-in frustration—a doubly important answer, since through it the child who came in second, in the thousands, might some day make up the audiences for performances by the first child.

The need we are considering represents more than stimulation, more than pride of achievement —important as they can be. At heart it is a social need. Private teaching and private studying can be extremely lonely activities. This is particularly true of the piano because it is the most self-sufficient of the popular solo instruments, and while enjoying it may be gregarious, piano study and practice require a somewhat aloof isolation. By its very completeness, its independence, and the extraordinary wealth of its literature, the piano can be the most secluded of all experiences.

For this reason, perhaps, virtually all the famed piano pedagogues of former days (less difficult but more demanding) set regular sessions, once or twice a week, when their pupils gathered to play for each other. Following their playing, they would submit to the master's comments and even to each other's outspoken reactions. Invariably, these "master-classes" were vibrant affairs.

I enjoyed years of such invaluable evenings weekly in my later teens when I studied in New York with Ernest Hutcheson, the Australian-British pianist and scholar, who became the first dean of the Juilliard School. Every Wednesday evening, his many pupils would gather at his home, knowing that "Hutchie" might call upon any of us without warning to try some of our repertory before audiences of unpredictable brilliance.

Such group therapy was not only good for handling nervousness in public playing, but it was also an opportunity to learn and become familiar with a huge literature. Hutchie's comments on interpretation were brilliant, firm, and unequivocal. During the informal fraternizing over lemonade and cookies that followed, he gave his students unintended yet invaluable lessons in hospitality, deportment, and speech. At the same time and place, treasurable associations and friendships were begun. There one saw George Gershwin and John Erskine, and Olin Downes, music critic of the *New York Times*, who were all "unofficial pupils" of Hutchie's. One might walk in on Josef Hofmann or Josef Lhevinne, Fritz Kreisler or Leopold Stokowski, their ears and eyes inspiringly attentive to every note played, every word uttered.

One evening at Hutchie's when I was about eighteen, I was called upon to play a few works by Chopin and Rachmaninoff. Luck was with me and things went quite well. Later, during the refreshment period, a modest and soft-spoken gentleman came up to me and said, "Thank you. You made me forget everything except what beautiful music that is." He, on the other hand, made me remember everything about that evening, especially the kindness, generosity, and courtliness that Irl Allison always radiates. Though no more than twenty-five at the time, he seemed to me an almost patriarchal figure, and it was not at all surprising to learn that he was already a dean of fine arts.

Almost all his life, Irl Allison has lived in the academic world, and early learned how weak our educational system was and still is in the study of the fine arts. And he knew other things, as a pianist and piano teacher: how important it is to make of music something above and beyond a painful, dull, and lonely grind; how discouraging can be the "perfectionist" standards of professionalism that may be thrust at the student before any real motivation for self-discipline has been established. Finally, and perhaps most importantly, he wondered what sense it made to develop artists to go out and starve. He knew that an audience must be prepared for them, and that the best way to create audiences is to train them. The most ardent music-lover is the man who plays or sings a bit himself—just as the staunchest baseball fan is the kid who has been a hero or a bum on his own sandlot team.

In fact, when in 1929 Irl Allison as dean of fine arts at Hardin-Simmons University founded the National Piano Playing Auditions, they were organized along the lines and philosophies of noncompetitive sports events in which each satisfactory entrant received some award commensurate with his achievement. This was a mechanism to provide enormous incentives: students were stimulated to compete for goals and awards because they were not competing against each other but against standards of their own.

Not even Allison could have foreseen that from this modest beginning, which forty years ago attracted forty-six entrants to the tiny town of Abilene, Texas, would emerge the largest organization of music teachers in the world—whose membership ranges from public school music teachers to internationally eminent musicians, whose "auditions" are now entered by about 70,000 pupils in 700 centers across the continent.

The National Guild of Piano Teachers is structured so as to encourage a joyous, enriching envi-

ronment in the studios of its members, many of
whom serve as judges for other cities in annual,
noncompetitive auditions. The few specifications as
to repertoire stress both quality and range: something of Bach is expected, and the program should
include classic, romantic, and modern material; the
judges have an eye out, too, for contemporary
American composers.

Standards of difficulty run the gamut from the
one memorized piece, scale, and cadence required
for the pledge member's certificate (a special in-
ducement for beginners who are slow, or timid, or
who have trouble memorizing) to the Brewster-
Allison $1,000 Piano Award Contest, sponsored by
the guild jointly with the Austin (Texas) Symphony
Orchestra, and involving a full solo recital plus performance of two concertos with orchestra.

Capping even these is the quadrennial Van Cliburn International Piano Competition, with a more
diversified sponsorship including the guild with its
top prize of $10,000. The last three contests men-
tioned are of course competitive; but the long suc-
cession of twenty-six more modest projects, among
which the latest are special Bach and Sonata med-
als, ask of the student—and the teacher behind
him—only that he do justice to the music he has
chosen and to his own progressing skills. If money

is a problem, incidentally, the guild offers cash scholarships to deserving applicants—more than fifteen hundred of them have been given since 1950.

Walter Merchant, editor of the bimonthly *Guild Notes* magazine, is of the opinion that the organization "has done for the average student in the musical part of his life what public education has done for the general education of all students." Also culled for this book is a typical comment from a veteran teacher-member.

"The teachers themselves find that being engaged in a common endeavor and guided by the guild precepts develops a camaraderie which substitutes personal contention for contention as to who can do more for his students. . . ."

The guild also sponsors a recording competition that offers a grand prize of $1,000 and ten other cash prizes. The standards are extremely high, for the final prize can only be competed for by the first winners in every category. To Irl Allison, music is the strongest symbol of mankind's spirituality, reflecting an inner peace and power diametrically opposed to the in-fighting of the profession struggle. He wants everyone to find the beauty and strength that lie within music, to integrate musical and human experience, and to assert the creative principle that will sustain mankind in all of its tribulations.

As individuals—teachers, students, performers—we must be receptive enough to let music describe to us the ultimate truth of existence.

Such a teacher, apparently, taught Neil Armstrong's mother, who in turn brought about appreciative music-making in her family. And so, in due course, the first man to make footprints in space took along a living musicality. How do we value that sort of equipment, for him? Is it more, or less, than the new car or the indispensable color TV? I think Armstrong has answered all these questions and inspiringly. And so has Phyllis George from Denton, Texas, Miss America of 1970, who declared that the joy of piano-playing and the disciplines that enabled her to win several guild awards contributed importantly to her national victory.

Two recent developments assure the continuation of the guild's life along similar lines for at least another generation: its designation by the federal government as an educational institution, and the election of the founder's able son, Irl Allison, Jr., as president.

The guild's basic philosophy was the model for my own project *Musical Talent in Our Schools,* a series of auditions and radio programs offered first in 1950 by the *New York Times* and its radio station WQXR, and continued for a dozen years. It provided for the nomination by New York high school principals or music supervisors of talented pianists, violinists and cellists to play in preliminary auditions and then, if qualified, before a panel of eminent musicians—among whom in one year were Jascha Heifetz, Vladimir Horowitz, Artur Rubinstein, Rudolf Serkin, Leonard Rose, and Leonard Bernstein. Those who had been approved played and were interviewed by me in a series of Sunday afternoon broadcasts. For all the high professional caliber of our jury, professionalism as such was incidental—almost accidental, you might say, though a number of splendid artists first found the limelight through this project. Basically, it was on behalf of the amateur: to encourage youngsters toward musical participation as an essential and enjoyable part of their general education, to stimulate standards of excellence, and to make the public at large aware that such gifted people were in their midst. And the response was invariably exciting.

By the way, when the sponsors of professional competitions asked me to "intercede" on their behalf to obtain the services of these judges—who were paid nothing—the judges usually declined. Why? Because our project was truly educational, not aimed to create more struggling artists but more music lovers to support art and artists. A musical nation is a nation of amateurs. No professional musician who is not in his heart overwhelmingly an amateur in the best sense—a lover of what he is doing—will ever establish the rapport with an audience which is the *sine qua non* of all public favorites, whose concerts are a human as well as musical experience. In the classical field, very few have the personal magic that creates frenzied adulation. In the popular field, if you don't have it, you are no place at all. And what is "it" exactly? Recently, Peter, Paul, and Mary were talking quietly about "it" and about their feelings toward music, towards their public. Thankfulness was their primary emotion. Peter wants to "hug all the beautiful people who have blessed me by coming to hear the concert."

Paul says: "The reason we play and sing is to further the Second Commandment: Love Thy Neighbor. I'm not ashamed to say that my goal is to save the world. So many troubles between people are only reflections of troubles inside those people. True communication of thought and emotion for all men is our deepest hope."

Mary says, "Yes, don't you see, that's what it's all about. Music is a way of achieving it. We sing to ourselves when we are alone. We sing to each other or listen to music together or make music together in the knowledge that the sharing of sound makes us all belong to each other, enables us to give all of ourselves in every way we can, with all the feeling

146

we have inside. That's communication."

Edwin Black once wrote of them: "It is because they are one that their common philosophy is communicated with such strength. You sit and listen, until suddenly your ears no longer hear, and your heart begins to feel."

Of course. And in my "strictly classical" days, this sense of art was possessed by a chosen few—Paderewski, Kreisler, Caruso, Toscanini, Bori, Farrar, Flagstad, Rachmaninoff, Casals, Rubinstein and a handful of others. But in the popular world, it belonged to every idol—from Louis Armstrong to Rudy Vallee. I've counted carefully to eighty-seven names that leap to my memory, including Jolson, Gershwin, Chevalier, Bea Lillie, Gertrude Lawrence, Fanny Brice, Benny Goodman, Glenn Miller, Paul Whiteman, Duke Ellington, Ella Fitzgerald, Crosby, Sinatra, Merman, and who couldn't go on and on? That too says worlds.

I labor the point to place blame where blame belongs, on an obsolescent Establishment that equates *communication* with *commerce,* isolates itself within an insolent and insoluble mystique, acknowledges little of the current human temper or of the time, and spurns what it allows itself to recognize.

This sterile denial of the senses has been strongly responsible for society's absurd attitude that *art* is a solemn intellectual experience distinct from, indeed opposed to, unalloyed delight. Such joyless and false values also supply reasons why our national potential as a society of art-music fans receded so alarmingly, despite the guild and other organizations with identical or similar objectives.

Also battling our esthetic problems are several other organizations of instrumental teachers, for string-players, guitarists, wood wind and brass musicians, and church organists. Fervently, we wish them the comparable administrative fortune and numerical strength of the Piano Teachers Guild to dig at the roots of our troubles.

Earnestly helping to shepherd the hundreds of small civic and community orchestras across the country is the National Symphony Orchestra League, for twenty-seven years under the tireless leadership of its Executive Director Helen Thompson, who now manages the New York Philharmonic.

In another healthy development, musical organizations here and there are inviting the public to sing-along performances of choral masterworks; the Princeton (town) Society of Musical Amateurs, for instance, schedules an annual series of concerts including composers (in 1969–70) from Bach to Gilbert and Sullivan to Poulenc, and the nation is teeming with such events.

All these incitements to amateurism grow from

148

deep American roots. The first widely known composer on these shores, William Billings, made his living as a tanner; Thomas Jefferson was an avid quartet player, as are a number of notables in this century; Charles Ives wrote most of his music in the time spared him by a successful and creative career in insurance; the Philadelphia lawyer Henry Drinker shared his insatiable love of Bach (in particular) with the innumerable congregations of singers and players that gathered weekly at his home.

To these people, music was as serious a thing, in what they got from it and gave to it, as it is to any full-time "career" musician. But their kind of seriousness was quite different from the pretentious, joyless artiness with which "serious" musicians, especially the serialists, have alienated not only young audiences, but their elders.

The healthiest result of the Establishment's destructive insistence that music is primarily an intellectual activity which must be *understood to be appreciated*, is the obvious resentment aroused within the dropouts, who answer in effect: "So— only the educated elite can penetrate the mystique of your music? Jazz and rock and pop are beyond the pale? OK man, go stew in your sterility."

This is a legitimate reaction to the corrupting immunity from open competition and communicative responsibility that the Establishment enjoys,

especially at university music departments. The entire situation has become so openly ridiculous that
perhaps we are on the brink of the final destruction
of what Henry Pleasants termed "impotence, impudence and incompetence unexampled in the annals of mankind." But nothing precipitated the
decline of academicism so swiftly as its neglect of
the provocative youngsters, especially those of the
sixties, who demanded from art not the scent of
prestige but rather the excitement and meaning and
passion to which they could respond.

This is among the many things that the world of
"serious" music has yet to learn, to absorb, and to
take to heart. And among the pleasantest is the
realization that there are today almost as many musical amateurs (potential customers, to hammer the
point) with genuine catholicity of taste, as there
are students in our high schools, colleges, and universities. It is as natural for them to strum a guitar,
hum a tune, tootle on a recorder, pick out a melody
on the piano, and to sit in with the school orchestra, chorus, glee club, band, or small dance combo,
as it was to play baseball or tennis or bridge.

Theoretically (and I wish I could say in actual
fact), the adequately trained instrumentalist should
find as much to do as he cares to do whenever
and wherever there are enough dubs whose pleas-
ures include playing music, hearing music, any and

150

all music from Palestrina to pop and discovering that some of it sticks to the ribs, and a lot doesn't.

Yes, music can be a luxury, an entertainment for royalty. King Saul of Israel could call on David to soothe him with it; Alexander the Great could swoon to it; Prince Charles of England can summon Yehudi Menuhin and thirty-two strings to his Buckingham Palace coming-of-age party; Princess Irene of Greece can make for herself a bona fide pianistic life. But in the contemporary instances at least, the real splendor of music is a human splendor—the joy of realization—and its sole criterion the quality of disciplined expressivity.

Whether or not any one person needs such a noble, humane, and sustaining phenomenon, it is all too clear that the world does.

9

A Look at the Record

Our contemporary musical life would have intrigued Ralph Waldo Emerson, who if alive today might well retitle one of his best known essays "The Plurality (rather than The Duality) of Life." Certainly, he would be drawn to examine it and perhaps to conclude that in so capricious a field as music, figures and facts, even statistics, are mischievously misleading. This, at any rate, is what I conclude from my own experiences, supplemented in the last few years by considerable roaming and snooping.

From the concert organizations, managers, and publicists, there has come a steady crescendo of distress. Ticket sales are indeed drastically down, even for famed organizations and big-name soloists. The combination of smaller income, rising costs, and prohibitive production and operating overhead spells potential bankruptcy for many in the concert business.

The idolized Leonard Bernstein, perhaps the most successful musician of our time, has predicted that "conventional symphony concerts will inexorably become museum pieces for the younger generation." The word "conventional" is the clue to his meaning. In our time, convention is indeed doomed, and good riddance. Others insist that concerts have calcified because of more practical factors: inadequate or no subsidies; high ticket prices; people's fear for personal safety after dark; traffic congestion, and transportation difficulties in general; oversupply of entertainment, even for free. Most of these conditions are urban-bred. New York as the musical capital of the world suffers most and yet paradoxes abound.

High ticket prices? The toughest ticket in town to get is precisely the most expensive—$35 a pair at

153

the Met. Unsafe streets? None is so dangerous as a park path, yet evening performances by the New York Philharmonic Orchestra and the Metropolitan Opera in the parks of the five boroughs draw up to 100,000 people, who begin to gather five hours before curtain time.

Logic is not life. And it certainly isn't the concert life. As Artur Rubinstein once said, "Who could ever explain why audiences turn out in droves or stay away?" But perhaps failure is less difficult to analyze than success, if one is willing to face facts. Not many are, you know.

Publicist Alix Williamson, a keen observer, is an exception. "I'm pretty tired of hearing this whining about the public's declining interest in classical concerts," she says. "I think it's the participants and the promoters who are really declining. The same old tired people, doing the same old tired things in the same old tired way. Is *that* any way to attract *today*'s masses?"

Pianist Leonard Pennario also has his fingers on the public pulse, judging by his penetrating answer to my question whether he himself had experienced the widely reported drop in engagements or in paying customers.

"Not personally," he said, touching wood, "but I'm not unaware of the gloomy accounts and rumors. You know, I've been wondering how much of this might not be the fault of artists themselves. Why are concerts such solemn affairs? Why shouldn't we aim to make them vital events, exciting events, and therefore really popular events? What kind of twentieth-century idiocy is it that made 'popularity' such a deadly sin? It's musically so naive, when you think of the great nineteenth-century composers and performers and the popularity they sought so eagerly—and attained! Somehow, our century's cultural clique actually shuns that.

"Yet something's happening. It's hard to put the finger on, but it's in the air all right. Just look at the tremendous new public available today, all under thirty, full of restlessness and curiosity. But they'll only go 'where the action is,' as they put it. Well, let's face it—how much 'action' can you get at the average concert or recital? What one finds so often is a routine program—classic or romantic or modern is not the point. I mean plain dull—a deadpan formality of presentation and an apathetic exit on a scattering of applause. There's been too much of that for too long. Audiences won't buy it any more. Why should they?"

They shouldn't and they won't. Of course the magical stars and the prestigious ensembles will always be there, performing at top prices in huge halls packed to the beams. But except for their performances, it is widely held, the halls are growing

155

depressingly empty. Even the subscribers to prepaid series stay away in hordes. The hard-core, old-guard music lovers are shrinking numerically.

I don't question that. But the reasons are correctable, because they have nothing to do with any diminution of people's love and need for music. Never before in its history has music been so permeating a part of the life of so great a percentage of the world's plain citizens.

And never have there been so many estimable musicians, not excluding solo performers, who despite the fact that most are not box office magnets, are nevertheless enjoying fruitful careers, appearing on numerous concert series and with orchestras in the intellectual and social centers of all the continents year in and year out. They command fees ranging from $250 to $2,500. They play from fifty to ninety concerts a year. One can no longer refer to a concert "season," because the proliferation of amphitheaters and festivals, and of jet planes that shuttle artists from city to city, coast to coast, continent to continent, have made the formerly relaxing summer interval an equally hectic time for about one hundred and fifty highly successful soloists who are heard regularly in the United States.

Despite all the professional griping, one must acknowledge this as among the few positive aspects of music-making today. Right on the most treacherous terrain of all, the solo field, there is the largest number of performers in history enjoying unprecedented opportunities.

To be sure, the number is puny, but not too long ago almost all of these superbly equipped soloists would have had few or no chances to perform publicly. Many of them would have been teaching in order to stay in music and to support their families. Others would have struggled to find a meager supply of jobs in orchestras or radio stations, movie houses, restaurants, or dance halls. The rest would have quit, compelled to find some more merciful means of earning a livelihood.

A dozen short years ago, the musical scene was far more depressing, when the last "live" group of musicians was fired from a "good music radio station" that was the last broadcasting refuge for the classical artist. Before that, the non-soloists and the orchestral hopefuls who had discovered that even a "steady job" meant working only part-time, had been successively driven from movie houses, vaudeville theaters, and the dine-and-dance places. At that time, there were over a quarter of a million members of the Musicians' Union. The so-called full-time jobs, yielding an average of twenty-six working weeks per year, were divided between approximately twelve thousand instrumentalists, in major and secondary symphonies, opera and ballet

157

companies, and/or in making free-lance recordings and electric transcriptions.

For a magazine piece of 1967, I reminded the reader: "As for the would-be soloists of a decade ago, the music business had become ruthlessly restricted. There was room at the top, which the solo musician could almost never reach through any normal process of growth and development, as in virtually any other field of endeavor. There was room at the bottom, from which less than a handful ever escaped. In between, was no man's land."

For the performing musician who does not make a solo career, either from circumstances or choice, the happiest job-hunting lies in orchestral territory. The huge majority of jobs open there are available to string players, for obvious reasons, just as the fewest are available to pianists. But there are few ensembles that are not almost as desperately in need of fine players of all instruments as they are of the money to pay them. The number of first-desk jobs open at this moment is astounding. I phoned Local 802 in New York a few minutes before writing this. There was an opening for a first oboist of a splendid orchestra, not rated among the Big Five, salary: $15,000 plus. "And in that town, there are plenty of plusses," said the girl. There were sixteen fiddle openings, ranging from a minimum of $12,-000 to $20,000. The first figure is the New York

Philharmonic's minimum, for fifty-two weeks of employment. The second, the bonus salary offered for a first French hornist, again not by the Big Five. There were other openings for cellists, clarinetists, flutists, percussionists—sixty-two in all, none more than a few hour's distance from Big Town.

The "plus" is usually found in extra-orchestral activities, for limited indeed is the city that does not boast one or more colleges, universities, conservatories, or a cultural center. At any of these institutions worthy of the name, a musician will find ever-expanding artistic and educational programs for which qualified artists are needed to function in at least some advisory or pedagogical capacities. The college campus today is the largest consumer and dispenser of musical art, not only buying 75 per cent of professional activities of the United States, but also producing full-length operas, concerts, ballets, plays, chamber groups, and soloists in a vast project to train talented instrumentalists, singers, and conductors for the platform. And not only young Americans are there, but also the largest group of foreign students sent to any one country for a musical education.

The United States is therefore a Mecca for pursuing a musical career, especially a pedagogical one. A central concern of contemporary American life is precisely education, and the major institutions for defining that life and for shaping its goals are the liberal arts colleges and the universities. The pedagogical opportunities are unlimited, for the fundamental weakness of university music study is the shortage of great teachers who are also attuned to the social and musical revolutions raging around them. Too few are able to alert the student to the needs and challenges confronting him, or even to recognize and utilize them as promising opportunities.

Why then, in this land of milk and honey, do so many insist that the musician and the musical career are in sore straits? Let me count the ways, or some of them, in which the world of classical music is experiencing difficulties. Perhaps it may be of aid in arriving at some constructive conclusions.

In any estimation of what's happening in music today, how it got that way, and how the musician is faring, it may seem odd to turn first toward the recording industry. Yet, no segment of the musical art and business has recognized and documented to so astonishing a degree every phase of our century's mercurial methods of creating, performing, and reproducing sound. Few have lived closer to or participated more in its recent development, especially its electronic growth, than John McClure, Director of Columbia Masterworks. In *High Fidelity*, he traces the course of a revolution which the "serious musical Establishment" knew virtually nothing about and, what little it did know, swept under the rug.

"Do you remember how it was?" Mr. McClure asks. "Prosperity was real. . . . The number of symphony orchestras and opera companies was growing. Music education was improving . . . the New Leisure would create the New Culture. . . . Our kids would share with us the glory of Bach, the power of Beethoven, the anguish of Mahler . . . we would have Lincoln Centers all ready for them.

"Ah, how carefully we prepared their new world. Then came rumors of a plague of Beatles . . . the cracks began to appear. The plague became an epidemic. Slowly, the dimensions of the generation gap . . . CHASM . . . became clearer. We couldn't understand them and they weren't listening to us. The bitter truth was they didn't want the world we had prepared for them and they didn't *need* our music; they were too busy making their own. . . . Record sales were booming, but *theirs,* not ours. . . . Where did we go wrong? Every classical musician asked himself that . . . or should have.

"There is no sense in minimizing the crisis that faces classical music and, by extension, classical recordings." McClure disclosed that in the decade 1958–68 overall sales of classical records declined 17 per cent. Over the same period, popular record sales increased 300 per cent, bringing the last total annual take up to $1.25 billion! The kids ignited this explosion. According to McClure, "As the old classical record buyers die, they are *not* replaced by their children. It takes no brains to draw stern conclusions from this."

Perhaps not, but the statement stands as a frightful indictment of the classical musical world, for every phase of it today reveals that "no brains" is considerably more than the Establishment has been using to evaluate and amend its archaic and stagnant condition. Particularly obnoxious has been its snobbish indifference to the vital ferment taking place outside its privileged environs.

No sooner had I set down McClure's statement than the old argument flared up again, hotter than ever, this time aggravated by the increasingly disastrous situation of classical record sales.

The current stone-casting comes from the 1970 Pulitzer Prize-winning composer Charles Wuorinen, who charges the large companies with "suicidal unawareness . . . of having packaged and repackaged the same handful of musical pieces from the past. The miracle is that they could get away with it for fifty years, not that they are in trouble now. Where is their responsibility to their own time? Why have they not tapped, and then massively promoted, the serious music of the present?" he asks.

The unwillingness of the experimentalists to realize that decades of wallowing in the mire of noncommunication has left them without any public; their inability to face reality or to read a balance sheet leaves them living a fantasy life in limbo, sputtering bitter charges that have little validity.

The phrase "suicidal unawareness" applies even more accurately to the so-called cultural institutions in the world of classical music than to the commercial organizations whose survival depends upon public demand and support. It fits perfectly the record companies' misguided attempts to discharge their self-assumed custodial obligations in spite of an infinitesimal "demand"; it also applies to the shortsighted policies of the musicians' unions, which have priced our symphonic and operatic groups out of the running.

But most of all, the phrase applies to a generation of composers which has finally and totally, it now appears, alienated the most tolerant public in history. And the future looks bleak unless the esthetic and educational cliques renounce their vanity and their distorted values.

For almost a century, composers and performers, and the moneymen of music, with too few exceptions, have been working in a professional vacuum. "And the critics," says Henry Pleasants, "will not get off their beat to find out what has been going on in music for the past century." The concertgoers and the record buyers have long been turned off from "modern" music by generations of experimentalists who have no desire or need to communicate. The avant garde has thereby created a derrière garde whose enthusiasm and support are reserved for Rossini revivals and the umpteenth performance of Tchaikovsky's *First Piano Concerto.*

It does sound brainless, in view of the highly advertised "cultural explosion." What's happened to *that,* by the way? Don't ask. Just observe or inquire around to discover how many of its most conspicuous symbols, those gleaming crystal-and-marble cultural centers, those gaudy, glassy palaces whose constructions have broken the financial backs of cities from ocean to ocean, are now filled by silence. Some are aired out a few times a year, others are not staffed or utilized at all.

Obviously, the money spent on these ornate mausoleums would have been more wisely used to stimulate creative, interpretive and administrative talents in the community, to foster young individuals in pop groups, to sponsor drama and ballet

and films, as well as opera and orchestra performances. Why wasn't it? Ah, that would have taken
vision, a less grandiose and more practical vision—
even harder to find than money, which itself is
becoming harder and harder to acquire in sufficient
quantity.

A viable center requires both imagination and
money. Just witness our pathetically few opera
houses and our many great symphony orchestras
including the Big Five of Boston, Chicago, Cleveland, New York, and Philadelphia, which are in
such real distress. So is the model of all our cultural institutions, Lincoln Center.

Is that because the audiences are dwindling?
Only partially. Even those that operate frequently
to sold-out subscription houses at alpine prices for
all performances are at this moment facing the
frustrating fact that the gap between the overhead
of any cultural organization and the money that
can be raised to meet it has now stretched to an
unbridgeable extent. The financial gap is practically
unbearable and it can only grow wider within our
economic structure. Some organizations are contemplating merger, or at least cooperation. Others
must simply fold, especially as audiences and record royalties continue to shrink.

Federal funds for the arts have been increased,
but only from peanuts to popcorn by the short-

sighted and Pentagon-panicked legislature of the richest nation on earth. Who else is to blame? One hardly knows where to point the finger. Plato said that what is honored in a country will be cultivated there. As a nation, we have never established the principle which every other civilized country, even the tiniest and the poorest, has long recognized: that government has a vested interest in subsidizing and promoting the arts, for they are not and can never be profit-making organizations, no matter what they do.

The separation of Art and State in our land is part and parcel of the provincial view of art as a decorative rather than as an integral element in everyday life. How can we expect more than token gestures from American legislatures when American journalism and even education share this basic disbelief in the value of art to society? But did we not mention with pride some splendid music departments in our schools and colleges and universities? For each of these fortunate institutions, however, there are hundreds of others that are so lacking in standards, so empty of teachers worthy of the name, that they would do better to have no music departments at all. Only a few years ago, Columbia University's national survey of institutional pedagogy led to the unequivocal conclusion that music is "the worst taught subject in the United States."

Nevertheless, it is not only low standards and inept teaching which are at the root of a poor music curriculum. Just as often, one finds in a teaching job a highly accomplished musician whose perspective is as deeply based in the past as the repertory he teaches. I've seen dozens of excellent performers working as artists-in-residence who have frankly confessed that they have lost their hold on the interest and confidence of their students. What our universities need urgently are teachers to train and *re*train other teachers: inspiring educators who are not only idealistic musicians but also realists alert to the needs of their students and the challenges each and every one must meet to conduct their studies and their lives intelligently.

Such teachers, while arming a pupil to the teeth, will also caution him that no amount of even the most advantageous study is a substitute for personal observation and experience; that in a time of such revolutionary ferment as ours, just about everything is bound to be in a mess; that music is merely one of many studies that must be radically reassessed; and finally, that the fact that we may not have immediate remedies for the ills of our world is no reason for discouragement. Right now, the cultural

167

Establishment is basically optimistic despite the financial troubles that are mounting annually. It argues that the problems are mainly monetary; that our nation is the musical center of the world; that more and better music is now available than ever before; that the potential audiences for it are enormous; and that more money is being spent for music and made from music than at any period, anywhere in the world.

True. For the moment. But these blessings have not been unmixed. The marvelous technological advances that have enabled a geometrically growing audience to hear music, have also contributed to making it progressively less possible for the average musician to earn a living by playing it. And while the musical boom has stimulated musical study and ambition and the development of a huge number of competent musicians, the number of musical jobs has been relatively decreasing.

At the moment, we do have more orchestras, more ballet companies, and even more opera companies than ever. But all of them are living on their knees, staring at astronomic deficits. The officials of labor have been as shortsighted as the officials of management. Their demands on nonprofit cultural organizations that are running expensive entertainment at inevitable losses are threatening one after another with nothing short of bankruptcy. And

168

this is not because cultural activities attract a pathetically small minority of the population. The simple question remains: where will the money come from? Even the flourishing recording companies have had to abandon almost all domestic recordings of operas and symphonic works to meet the competition of foreign markets.

Radio is a forest of recordings, TV a sea of musical mediocrity, primarily of pop singers who cling to a microphone as to a life raft. The music for all the films made is put on sound tracks by a few dozen musicians, superlative sight-readers and virtuosos who make fortunes and so are zealously holding down the hardest-to-get of all commercial jobs.

A dismal picture? Indeed, but not so dismal as its primary cause—the crippling war that has diverted our money and our efforts from constructive and cultural activities into bigger and better ways of killing. The only answer to esthetic survival today is subsidy, just as the only answer to human survival is peace.

Obviously, the problems that beset classical music pertain mainly to what music lovers in every part of the world call "good music"—European-oriented classical music of the past three centuries. And perhaps nothing reflects the dichotomy of the American musical scene more than the fact that

169

this music thrives in a country whose national sport, so to speak, is a jazz music that began to evolve early in this century entirely unrelated to the European idioms.

As noted earlier, the cultural Establishment always regarded jazz, in all its manifestations, as something not quite literate or respectable, something entirely opposed to "good music." So the Establishment could hardly have welcomed rock 'n' roll when it burst upon the scene in the mid-1950s. This raw and sexy music was an affront to almost all adults, on three significant grounds: it was a rebellious reaction to the pabulum that pop had become, it was a hysterical haven for beatniks, and its heroes were the offensive and threatening vanguard of the teenage revolt.

Who could have predicted its staying power, its vital part in music becoming a billion-dollar business with unprecedented audiences and customers for everything that revolves around "rock"? This time, the Establishment was not alone in behaving like ostriches or in its fervent hope and expectation that this craze, too, would soon pass.

Instead, it has blossomed into our own thing, and rapidly spread around the world. Today it is regarded as an indigenous American contribution to musical evolution. To several hundreds of million people in every corner of the globe, it has become a way of life. And perhaps this is the stern fact that has at last compelled the Establishment to observe the capacity of this musical idiom to nourish the requirements of a gigantic public. At least it knows now that its own experimental wing has failed utterly to satisfy the appetite of the musical public. This is a promising development.

The transitional phase is being evidenced everywhere, and as this is being written, in the most unexpected places. In order to take cognizance of "the outside world," Gunther Schuller introduced during the summer of 1969 a series of concerts at Tanglewood that extended a trend already successfully started in the musical bastions of Boston. Featured at the staid Berkshire Festival was the rock singer, Janis Joplin, the gospel singer Mahalia Jackson, the folk singer Joni Mitchell, and jazzman Ornette Coleman. "We must change," Mr. Schuller announced, "we must find a broader spectrum. It doesn't mean excluding the permanent elements of the past, merely the Tchaikovskys of today."

Attendance records were shattered at Tanglewood when a rock concert drew an audience of twenty-two thousand for the Who and the Jefferson Airplane, while average attendance for the Boston Symphony's regular summer concerts ran to about eight thousand.

171

Meanwhile, back in the sticks, the world's largest musical happening was staged at the Woodstock Music and Art Fair in Bethel, New York, which drew over three hundred thousand young men and women to hear the music of rock stars throughout a rainy August weekend in the Catskills.

During six Sunday afternoons in Mount Morris Park in the heart of New York's Harlem, another three hundred thousand people attended a "Cultural Festival" consisting entirely of rock entertainers and sponsored to the tune of $250,000 by Maxwell House Coffee and the Columbia Broadcasting System.

These are but a few examples of the remarkable march of rock, from the excesses of its infancy to its relative maturity of today. And there are others, no less revealing.

In the spring of 1970, I checked the previous year's attendance figures at Carnegie Hall with the veteran box office manager, Nathan Posnick. "Last season's take at our place?" he asked, shaking his head sadly. "Thirty per cent off. The big big boys still pull, but there are few, and they're getting fewer, and not being replaced . . . not by classical soloists or groups. No doubt about it, there's a declining excitement over the usual concert attraction.

172

"The feverish activity for years now mainly centers around the pop, rock, folk, and all the jazz-oriented music, stars, and combos. You should see the audiences—kids, all under twenty-five, storming our box office and waving fists full of big bills demanding the highest priced seats.

"No one seems to understand exactly what's going on. These kids are looking for something . . . personality, love, warmth, someone who speaks their lingo. All I know is that ten years ago, a Judy Collins or Bob Dylan or Donovan or Peter, Paul and Mary wouldn't have dreamt of staging their shows at Carnegie. Now, they and lots of others like them are selling like hotcakes here and everywhere, doing concerts as well as records and TV and films, coining millions! Only the classical music business is in trouble. Maybe it's the lack of publicity or not facing up to what people want and need. Of course, there's no problem with glamour boys, and girls, classical or pop, never with the artists whose very lives seem dedicated to communicating to their public, identifying with them, pouring love on them—like Belafonte or the Beatles or Bernstein." I couldn't help musing: "The three Bs of our generation."

Mr. Posnick threw open one of the ticket racks, for a concert by a great visiting orchestra one week off. "Just look at that," he cried, "Is that or isn't

173

that one of the top five orchestras in the whole world? And how often do they hit New York? Yet, you could paper an apartment with the unsold tickets. Now, look at this," he said, flinging another rack wide open. Two lonely tickets, singles, rested there. "And they're waiting to be picked up," he said. "For whose concert?" I asked. "For The Byrds," he answered with a grin, "and I'm not kidding. You know, the rock group. I can see by your face you're surprised, but try and get in! See what I mean?"

Of course one sees, but it has led to such simplistic suggestions for the "cure" of our ailing classical scene as the engagement of the most glamorous pop stars and groups as soloists with our symphony orchestras, the commissioning of rock operas by the Met, the organization of big rock bands in all our colleges, universities, and conservatories and cultural centers. And finally, the training of young musicians to include every aspect of Afro-American culture which may somehow significantly link the declining "serious" and frenzied "rock" worlds of music.

I would not be so rash as to assert there are unbridgeable gaps between any musical styles or idioms or forms—not after seeing the many mixtures and miscegenations in the wildly divergent strains in the other arts. But I would insist that if

174

any solid relation or cross-fertilization can develop, it will have to be along better lines and on firmer ground than what has heretofore been offered by the composers, interpreters, and expedient impresarios in both fields. With but a handful of exceptions, we have been handed preposterous circuses masquerading as the wave of the future. All they have provided is unmistakable evidence that the cults of culture and counter-culture are now but exhausted clichés, hanging on the ropes.

Every corner of the musical world needs to re-examine itself honestly: the poor and pathetic "revolutionaries" of the sterile classical avant garde; the performers and their diminishing audiences; the officials of the cultural centers, whose super-theaters are becoming mildewed while they ponder the question, year after year, of what on earth to put in them to remove the dampness and the dullness. And among the deans and faculties of most of the academic institutions I observed, there is a feeble show of keeping pace with a world they neither can grasp nor oppose. They are filled with a lack of self-confidence and a depressing realization of their irrelevance to today's techniques and values.

Turning back to the commercially successful rock establishment, it too must re-examine itself. Each day, another of its flamboyant specialties, its gimmickries, its pet synthesizers, its electronic sonorities of deafening decibels—all of this adds up to be less than the early hysterical rock fans proclaimed it to be—the magic catalyst that would restore this diseased and sorrowful world to health and happiness, that would attain for humanity the millennium.

At its peak, rock's creativity and energy and imagination were marvelously exemplified by the poetry and music of Bob Dylan, and especially by its masters, the Beatles, who anticipated and epitomized not only the Now Sound but also the Now Generation.

However, I am compelled to confess that a lot of hard listening, in the years since I expressed such high hopes for an eventual synthesizing of all musical techniques with rock as the strongest energizing component, has finally ended in skepticism.

Remember the inherent genius of the Beatles' 1966 LP *Revolver* and its subtle manipulation of raga rock; of their film *Yellow Submarine* and its psychedelic search into the shattering realities of existence? Remember Simon and Garfunkel's *Sounds of Silence*? And the 1967 Carnegie Hall mixed-media concerts of the New York Pro Musica (those dozen masters of medieval and Renaissance music) and the five-man rock group from the Electric Circus? These were among the buoy-

176

ant experiences that filled one with respect, that made one hope that a new art form was being evolved.

Instead, we have witnessed a series of disappointments: the pretentious TV program *Switched-On Symphony*; recording à la Baroque of impressive ineptitude; a couple of Carnegie Hall turkeys— lame attempts at aural integration such as Luciano Berio's *This Means That* and *The First Moog Quartet*. The former was a mishmash with an embarrassing commentary by a "cozy" president of a girls' college; the latter, an evening of utter amateurishness, almost enough to destroy the widely held expectation that the Moog synthesizer may well become the instrument of the new music. And to make the proceedings even more discouraging, it was the wily Sol Hurok who was entrapped into presenting the melancholy event.

The rock party may well be over. This opinion is shared by a man far more conversant with its history than I, Professor Albert Goldman, who recently wrote in the *New York Times*: "The latest albums of rock geniuses (the Beatles, Bob Dylan) show an unhappy drift toward purely commercial aspects of music. What is even more dismaying than this industrialization of the art is the acceptance of the bubblegum mentality by even the finest rock musicians. . . . As the ideals and myths that

177

had sustained rock began to crumble in 1967, into the gap rushed the banished swarm of parasite producers, impresarios and financial wheeler-dealers. In no time rock was computerized into the stalking zombie it is today, lurching along without a thought, a purpose or a plan beyond that offered by the record rating charts . . . not even asking, 'Where do we go from here?' "

Where *should* it be going? It should be resisting the easy money that has corrupted its ideals and standards, and developing its own musical structures; otherwise, it cannot evolve as an art of significance. Recognizing its "bag" for what it is, essentially a musical amalgam, rock should prove the most flexible of idioms. Once it achieves freedom from the rhythmic tyranny of the big beat, then it may unleash fruitful experimentation and a complete release of the creative spirit. Then would it be neither rock nor classical, but a totally new synthesis. It's an exciting prospect—if it works.

What, may we ask, has this to do with classical music? No one can answer that question with any certainty because we cannot tell what direction music will take.

Quincy Jones, among the best established jazz composers and arrangers with extensive classical training, says: "I believe that the best music being written in this country today is coming out of films." A great deal of it, certainly. Gene Lees of *High Fidelity* says: "While most of the new generation of film composers have backgrounds in popular music . . . jazz . . . and classical music, perhaps the most significant thing about them is that they are evolving with casual skill and growing confidence, a new music that partakes of all three traditions—and other traditions as well. More and more of our best popular music is coming from films, and if you look at the record industry sales charts in any given week, chances are that you'll find at least one motion picture sound-track album listed near the top—perhaps several. Sound-track recordings have become powerful factors in the commercial exploitation of pictures. . . ."

And, we may add, of the recording industry's most dramatic new element: electronic sounds. Formerly, almost all such sounds were directly produced from a guitar or a violin or a voice, and then treated to alteration by electronic manipulation. Today, fewer and fewer sounds derive from instruments or voices, and more and more are generated by purely electronic means, from the equipment itself. Columbia Records' *Switched-On Bach* is still the most astounding technimusical accomplishment in this genre to date. Its creators, Walter Carlos, a physicist and audioengineer, assisted by musician Benjamin Folkman, conceived the mad

179

and marvelous idea of creating a collage of J. S. Bach's catchy themes and treating them to all conceivable (and more than a few inconceivable) manipulations through the Moog electronic synthesizer.

How did Mr. Moog feel about the unprecedented reaction? "Electronic music," said its most imaginative contributor, "is at its awkward growing stage, its young adult period. People will have to settle down now and learn what can be done. That takes a long time."

In the meantime, the redoubtable Bach specialist, Rosalyn Tureck, devoted an entire lecture-recital at the Lincoln Center Library in New York to "Bach and the Electronic Media," playing one voice of Bach's *F Minor Sinfonia* on the piano against the other two voices that she had previously recorded on the Moog instrument. Obviously, "music as usual" is on its way out.

In the steady continuing effort to raise rock to the status of an art form, recordings no longer simply "reproduce" live performances. They have now assumed the dimension of independent productions, improvisational and self-sufficient studio creations in which electronic composers and engineer-technicians are increasingly synthesizing the materials of rock and serious composition.

Arnold Shaw, in his remarkable book, *The Rock*

Revolution, examines this trend and its implications: "From simple folklike songs, rock has moved into the area of extended forms. From albums consisting of disparate three-minute tracks, it has developed in the direction of the integrated suite and the musical theater. . . . It has become an instrument of commentary, introspection, analysis, satire, humor, irony and protest . . . and has brought a revival of bardic tradition—songwriters performing their own songs, poets chanting their verses to rock accompaniment. The blues, now sung to electronic instrumental background and embodying the Negro struggle for equality and freedom, has become soul—a more sensual, more violent and propulsive sound. . . . And now that the walls of musical segregation have come tumbling down, there is some indication that we may be on the edge of an integration in which composers will create, not pop, not rock, not folk, not art, but music that will embody the best qualities of each. . . ."

Perhaps. But certainly rock must be credited with tearing down the artificial boundaries, unique to our age, which segregated music into two categories—popular music, which was without prestige, and prestigious music, which was without popularity. I use the past tense in the fervent hope that enough of us have grown resentful enough of the

181

arrogant dichotomy to make it obsolescent once and for all.

The classical field has for too long sequestered itself in the deepest retreats of smug snobbery. The "serious" composers, teachers, performers, critics, concertgoers, and record buyers have been as wrapped up in their classical "husk" as an ear of corn (if they will pardon the expression). Finally, they are being compelled to face the music, and we may well be on the brink of the richest of all musical eras.

In the late sixties, while the classical recording graphs were plunging to new lows, the merchandising director of Columbia's Masterworks, R. Peter Munves, was producing albums whose phenomenal sales ran contrary to the downward trend of all other similar recordings. Utilizing a sturdy background of newspaper and trade magazine experience and especially of retail record-selling over the counter, and the possessor of a pair of unerring ears attuned equally to the cream of the classics and the cash register's highest "tessitura," Munves issued a series of smash hits, climaxed by the disk of the decade, *Switched-On Bach*. It constituted an historic recording feat not only technically, not only in sales, but also in the way it refused to fit any previously known musical category.

Upon Munves's appointment in 1970 as classical music director of RCA Records, his heartening statement of confidence that the prevailing problems in classical recordings were "fantastic, exciting, and conquerable challenges," sent me hotfooting it up to his new pad.

"Your optimism is refreshing," I said, "but just *how* do you propose to revive the same old enthusiasms?"

"Ah," said Munves with a winning smile, "that's *my* secret, though I trust it won't remain a secret for long. But I *can* tell you a few things. Nothing's 'the same old anything!' It's a brand new ball game today. You must merchandise not only a vital and viable product, but you must merchandise where the market *isn't*, not where it *is*.

"The age of buyers in the big potential music market is between twenty and thirty years. That's where you'll find the most imaginative and responsive music lovers, providing you meet their needs and desires. You've got to communicate to them clearly and directly or they won't dig you. Music, like everything else they call their bag, must be an intensified emotional experience, not an intellectual rite or a cultural void. Vacuums are not for them, and certainly not for us. I don't accept all the pessimistic evidence around. I think something can be done about it. More than something. It's already been proven, and we're going to keep on

183

proving it, more and more, by looking beyond the present repertories, by giving artists and groups and orchestras fresh images."

"One thing is clear," says Nat Hentoff. "The stereotypes of the past have all but disappeared. We are shooting the musical rapids—certainly a more enlivening experience than just contemplating the past in placid pools. And there can be as many destinations as there are travelers. It's all open now: no passports are needed; and everyone, player and listener, can make up his own itinerary—and keep changing it."

Perhaps no passports are needed, but plenty of time will be, and even more hard and realistic thinking. Spontaneous rebellion against the Establishment is no longer enough. Any further violent revolts are useless expenditures of energy that should now be used constructively. What we are actually witnessing is a mighty though as yet orderless effort to free man from every repressive, hypocritical, and unjust barrier of our own society. This is a noble cause, but it will be realized only when our wrath and bitterness begin to produce ideologies, organizations, methods, and results of our own.

None of us can afford to kid each other any longer. Much of the future of the entire world depends on these very issues. That means on the young people, and especially on young Americans.

184

Straws in the Wind

Although I have not yet heard any work by John Cage that places him among my favorite composers, I ran across something he said way back in 1937 that stamps him as my favorite prognosticator.

"I believe," he said, "that the use of noise to make music will continue and increase until we reach a music produced through the aid of electronic instruments. . . . Whereas in the past, the point of disagreement has been between dissonance and consonance, it will be, in the immediate future, between noise and so-called musical sounds."

An incredible stroke of vision! What makes it the more remarkable is the extent to which the prediction is now applicable to all music, and perhaps even more to concert music than to popular music.

Early in 1970, the Columbia-Princeton Electronic Music Center celebrated its tenth anniversary. The occasion was notable not alone for the fact that Charles Wuorinen's *Time Encomium* was awarded the first Pulitzer music prize ever bestowed upon a purely electronic composition, but also for proof positive that electronic music is a firmly established part of every aspect of our musical life.

Further festivities included the presentation of six concerts during a first-time Electronic Music Week, which featured the most significant compositions among the over two hundred that were created at the center by more than sixty composers from eleven countries. Nearly all had been publicly performed, and sixty-seven concert works by twenty-two composers are listed in Schwann's catalogue of recordings. Electronic scores have also enhanced countless movies, television productions, theater and dance presentations with an effectiveness as yet unmatched on the concert platform.

There was an exhilarating glow about the Columbia-Princeton events—except when the works themselves were being heard. Then rigor mortis appeared to seize entire audiences. Almost as soon as each piece began, a crushing solemnity would descend like a shroud over the entire proceedings. No one smiled, no one laughed, no one seemed to be enjoying himself at all.

And I don't mind admitting that I was the most depressed cat in the whole kennel.

Electronic Music Week set me to "take stock" all over again. There is no doubt that in electronicism the twentieth century has found a new medium to produce new music. But the search for newness is as old as the art of music itself. While Bach was consolidating the tonal system on which all Western music was built (except for the atonal compositions of our century), and while Beethoven was creating new edifices with almost every work, their contemporaries were busily devising new or improved music-making mechanisms. And these instruments, along with the great music written for them, were quickly embraced by the public.

Certainly, electronic music, whether produced through the synthesizer or the computer or merely through assembling and manipulating tape, has won such an appeal, so world-wide a popularity and influence, that only an ostrich could dismiss it as a passing fad. The utilization of this new medium,

especially on films and TV and recordings, is phenomenal. Its capacity for creating sounds, rhythms,
effects are limitless, surpassing anything previously
known to man or nature. But as concert fare—it is
still unappetizing.

And if that's the way the wind is blowing, it will
profit us to heed its direction. The blunt cool in
this case is that this new instrument's chief characteristic is its dehumanization. It eliminates the "interpreter," it allows the composer, like the painter
or the poet, to communicate directly with his audience. No longer does he need the performer or
"middleman," whose heartache or bellyache could
jeopardize the success or even the accuracy of the
performance.

There is no longer any need to speculate. Electronicism is here and has been for long enough for
us to take careful note of its presence, its impacts,
and their repercussions.

Thousands of compositions are listed in the available electronic music catalogues. Hundreds of records have been released—always a reliable barome-
ter of public acceptance. And now, the synthesizer
looms as the musical instrument in the parlor. Not
the quarter-of-a-million-dollar job which David
Sarnoff's Research Center at RCA constructed for
the Columbia-Princeton Laboratory, but the newer,

thousand-dollar models that a large number of people have recently bought.

Some of the feverish enthusiasm is undoubtedly due to the do-it-yourself factor built into the synthesizer. Anyone at all can become his own "Beethoven." Or so one is led to believe in an age of abstract paintings "created" by the tail of a chimpanzee—all seriously regarded, sizably priced, and sold out. Every field has its phonies; the good people and the good products survive. As for the charge that electronic music is essentially a commercial product because of the big money interests of the music world (movies, radio, TV, and recordings), this is a symptom of the same myopia that divided classical music and jazz so damagingly.

Electronicism has even accounted for a new awareness on the part of our academic institutions. At least, there are very few colleges and universities today that do not have some sort of electronic musical equipment which every music student is free to use. This is in contrast to the situation in Europe where the government-subsidized radio stations have been the primary patrons of electronic composition and performance.

Yet, even those who degrade electronic music to the status of "sound effects" should respect our academic institutions for investigating its potential.

If it does nothing but convince our educators that today one cannot teach the performing arts as merely major subjects in a liberal arts curriculum, that will be a healthy start.

To my mind, electronicism and rock suffered a setback when the British rock quartet The Who twice performed their "opera" *Tommy* on America's most sanctified stage, the Metropolitan Opera House. At that citadel of conventional uptightness, packed for the occasion by excited youngsters, an ambitious attempt was made to transcend the limitations of the standard rock shows.

This member of the audience left the performance a thoroughly disappointed and deafened man. The uncostumed cast (three instrumentalists and one vocalist) did their thing flanked by amplifiers juiced up to the nth degree of aural amplitude while they writhed about bathed in blinding spotlights that shifted from red to green to purple. There was no staging, no acting. The instruments bombarded the ears to the point of pain, and against such electronic blasting, the words were unintelligible, the plot incomprehensible.

So what made this an "opera"? Nothing. Nothing that happened at the Met, anyway, but a full year before this presentation, the group issued a

190

two-record album that was indeed operatic in every sense of the word. Here, the story is clear, credible, and contemporary. The music describes the dramatic action and supplies excellent opportunities for solo arias and choruses. The ear-splitting is reserved for intensely climactic moments. Elsewhere there is nuance and variety and tenderness, all of which were totally absent from the "live" version, don't ask why. The very meaning and beauty of this Christmas tale—with Tommy as the symbol of a humanity deaf, dumb, and blind to the essence of Christianity—were lost in the reckless roar of hard rock.

What charmed me was the audience. As the vanguard arrived, dressed in Indian headbands, multicolored slacks, black T-shirts, beads, medallions, Army jackets, pajamas, I heard the apprehensive comments of the Met staff. When the opera began, it became instantly apparent that from the recordings the kids knew every word that was being sung. I could not help thinking that in this great house of all houses, such a complete grasp of exactly what was going on at every instant was a rarity. And what else delighted me was the comment of an usher. "You know, sir," he said, "these kids are warmer and more genuine and much more polite than their parents who come here on 'their night.' They never fool us, and I'll never figure how they got such swell children."

Electronics is also writing the newest chapter in the evolution of the piano. The Baldwin Electric Concert Grand, a research model resulting from forty years of continuing experimentation, was promisingly launched by Lorin Hollander at a recital in the very bastion of rock, Fillmore East.

The instrument looks and sounds like a concert grand piano, and is played in the same manner. Differences consist of two additional pedals which can increase or decrease the dynamic range, and a separate control unit (directed by the pianist but operated by an engineer) which can vary timbre as well as volume. The instrument does not have a soundboard: the string vibrations are picked up by "ferro-electric cantilever transducers" (we are told), designed and patented by Baldwin.

Hollander's recital—a program including substantial works by Schubert, Debussy, and Prokofiev—attracted an audience of several thousand, from swooning hippies to hard-boiled moguls of music-biz, all of whom responded enthusiastically.

Whatever increases the tonal and coloristic spectrum of a major instrument is incalculably valuable to the whole cause of music, especially if it provides fresh inspiration and ever wider dimensions for composers.

And not only for those uniquely gifted creators we call composers, for today there is a connection, a breakthrough between the art of composing and the technique of producing sound electronically. Through that twentieth-century musical instrument, the tape recorder, even the imaginative non-musician can devise a mosaic of sound with its own validity.

During an orchestral rehearsal in Salzburg's Festspielhaus, a battery of scientists was at work trying to measure precisely how much electric current a conductor draws from his orchestra, what happens to his heart when the men don't start together, how high his blood pressure shoots when the French horn blows a blooper, and so on. Visitors could not believe their eyes when they discovered that the taped-up man with electrodes attached to his wired-up body was none other than Herbert von Karajan!

"And why should I *not* be doing this?" he asked, somewhat indignantly. "These experiments are meant to determine how we listen to music and what happens to us. What could be more important? I subscribe to the philosophy of the Beatles in *The Yellow Submarine*. If music is valuable enough for the Blues to steal from the Yellows, then it is valuable enough to cherish, important enough to feel deeply privileged to pass on its inspirational power to everyone. Now, how *does* one do that?"

On this side of the Atlantic, a video cartridge is being perfected which can be inserted into the home television set. The potential of this new device is unimaginable in its ability to change our entertainment and educational habits completely.

The possibility of purchasing or renting cassettes, of seeing and hearing whatever one wants whenever one wants, is now imminent enough to predict a revolution in the performing arts in all their dimensions, and at any moment.

What a century this is! First disks, then tapes, then cassettes, and now the combination of sight and sound in the home, where anyone can make like a movie star.

In a 1964 article on the Beatles, I wrote, "The musical and social awareness of this inspired quartet is comparable only to their imagination. Their easy assimilation and amalgamation of every style, from Elizabethan ballads to rock 'n' roll are totally individual . . . their beat is unique, their contribution historic."

The Beatles' barbed wit in verbalizing the ado-

194

lescent revolt was complemented by their harmonic and melodic vigor, inventiveness, and rhythmic force.

Later—around 1968—I noted ruefully an unmistakable concession to expediency and lowered standards of production and performance, and still later the weaknesses that their solo albums disclosed.

Together again in a new film and a new recording, *Let It Be*, the Beatles revealed an unmistakable diminution of their creative vitality. It was profoundly disappointing though not surprising, therefore, that with this release the Beatles announced their decision to disband, explaining that it had become difficult for them to create together and also grow individually. One remembers that "doing one's own thing" was always their credo. Yet it is ironic that the quest for an ideal should pose problems so formidable that the search was abandoned, especially by these contemporary troubadors, who once captured and dramatized so uniquely and imaginatively the griefs and joys, the miseries and beauties, the confusions and convictions of their era, our era.

None admired these qualities more than Bob Dylan, whose unique poetry was a clarion call to young people who found in him the truest prophet of their protest. They rallied round him in a nation-wide rebellion against a corrupt adult world. Dy-

195

lan's very first recorded song "Blowin' in the Wind," became the national anthem of the youth revolt. He has written the lyrics and music of some of the finest songs in American vocal literature. He created a new genre, folk rock, which added the rock fans to his prodigious folk-song following. Dylan's impact on the temper of our country has filled every politician with the pain of envy.

Then this canonized man released an autobiography—a two-disk album of twenty-four songs, only half of which are his own. An amiable anthology, it is also an astonishingly insipid collection of works and interpretations—a put-down or a put-on, a deliberate denial of the Dylan image. In this collection of bland folk, pop, and rock styles, the master of them all abandoned the austerities that belonged to the original stylist who once created a new landscape of true poetry with brilliant ferocity and compassion. Instead, there was a refined and resigned artist, a meticulous man satisfied with himself and with the world. Gone was the ferocity, gone was the cold anger, gone too were the rebellious, sardonic, and pathetic traits that distinguished his finest art.

There was a quaint ring to this retreat from activism while the war between the generations still raged and Dylan's old sarcasm could still be summoned: "Don't trust anyone over thirty." Characteristically, in subsequent recordings, Dylan himself

196

summoned his own integrity to produce remembrances of things happily not past.

As more and more fine musicians equally schooled in classical and jazz idioms enter the rock field, the ear-splitting volume is clearly on its way out, as exemplified by two American groups, the nine-man Blood, Sweat and Tears and the seven-man Chicago, and a five-man British group, The Moody Blues.

All three display artistic and technical finesse that belong only to musicians of the most expressive and expert quality. Especially their beauty of tone and sound, even in the midst of the most powerful climax, provides a crushing contrast to the unbuttoned vitality of the distortionists whose work soon becomes monotonous if not unbearable.

A tongue-in-cheek piece of rock entitled "Shell Game" accompanied the Offering at a jazz service one Sunday morning at St. Peter's Lutheran Church in New York. Before that, Clark Terry's big band had filled the edifice with the lush sounds of blues and jazz and folk hymns. Duke Ellington's spiritual, "Come Sunday," was the ecstatic finale. Performed with wild saxophone solos and exultant trumpets in cacophonous ensembles, the music brought the congregation to its feet in a burst of shouting fervor.

197

Somehow, it all added up to an intensified form of reverence entirely appropriate to this dauntless, mad, mod house of God.

Each new rock manifestation has produced fiery reactions, but none matched the hysteria that greeted the trend toward religious themes, mysticism, and spiritual ideals.

To the frantic fans, this is merely one more sign that rock is the symbolic medium of American youth's search for life's deepest values. To the skeptics, it is no more than another commercial gimmick as well as sheer blasphemy.

The trend seems to me a very natural rebuttal to rock's unhappy flirtation with drug lyrics, and a vitally needed expression of horrified reaction to the deaths through drug overdoses which had inescapable associations with rock stars, the lyrics they sang, and their effect upon the whole scene, stars and listeners alike.

But with a production such as the hour-and-one-half rock opera, based on the Passion and Death of "*Jesus Christ, Superstar*," one cannot question the sincerity and depth of its impulse regardless of one's opinion of the work. Simultaneous with its appearance on records, this imaginative and gaudily effective work by two young Englishmen, Andrew

Lloyd Webber and Tim Rice, was well performed and respectfully received at St. Peter's Church in New York. A sensational album sale led to the formation of two companies to tour in a concert version, whose smashing success motivated the transformation into an elaborate musical. It opened with the largest box office advance in Broadway history, and emerged as an eclectic, electric extravaganza, with another "E" for effort. Actually, it is a *pot-pourri moderne* by musicians who were evidently suckled on Buxtehude and grew up to admire Brubeck more. A straw in the wind it is, but not much more substantial.

Far more difficult for the music lover to reconcile is the new "synthesis" in which composers who insist that they are practicing the new mysticism and who profess the new romanticism are now enlisting the techniques of computers to realize their visions.

Evidently, creating what purports to be music has become an antimusical activity, to judge from the evidence of some hot-off-the-griddle recordings of computer music "realized" by various mathematicians, physicists, engineers, and spacemen. Composers they are not, if words mean anything they used to mean. What we hear are polyphonic textures of astonishing complexity; chordal clangings; up and down swirls and swoops of sound transferred

199

directly to tape rather than being produced by any conventional or electronic source.

The spectacular success of the Woodstock Festival led armies of promoters to organize and schedule similar events from coast to coast. A few came off well, some went terribly sour, but none matched the Woodstock extravaganza, for reasons ranging from inexperience to outbreaks of violence that brought destruction and sometimes death.

Inevitably resistance arose. Only a year after Woodstock, residents of Carbondale, Illinois, formed a Concerned Citizens group to fight a proposed three-day spring rock festival.

One citizen, however, a university professor, maintained that instead of seeing the rock festival as a threat, "we should see it as a great opportunity for southern Illinois to show the young world how understanding and sympathetic we really are." Perhaps that's what makes horse-racing; to what degree this attitude will overcome the mounting hostility toward rock festivals remains to be seen.

But there are other straws in the wind. At the Newport Summer Festival of 1970, no rock groups performed. Producer George Wein had announced before the festival that, "This will be a jazz year, because jazz fans now realize how close their music has come to being extinct. . . ." Joe Venute, Mahalia Jackson, and Dizzy Gillespie's quintet led a long list of New Orleans stylists, so "out" that they're "in." Who said jazz is dead? That's what they've been saying about "opry" for over three hundred years now.

So far as I am able to determine from a most contradictory set of "facts," jazz is neither dead nor is it being reborn and recharged with new vitality and success. It still has a loyal and loving audience. One could even call them fanatical devotees, for whom no other entertainment or art is comparable. Years ago, it was a colossal public and growing constantly. Today, it's a valiant little clique who could not keep their jazz idols in marijuana. All you have to do is to add up the number of bands, big or small, that are around today, the number of jazz soloists quite unable to find jobs or to make a living, and finally, just ask the record companies for the sad figures and facts. It reminds one all too painfully of what is happening in classical music.

Each year, splendidly supervised by Young Audiences Inc., some two hundred fifty professional musical groups perform about ten thousand informal playing-and-talking concerts before public school youngsters in thirty-four states, subsidized largely by the record industry's Music Performance Fund, the Leventritt Foundation, and federal grants.

The Phoenix Wind Quintet is well known among these groups for the provocative discussions it evokes. After playing some Vivaldi, its flutist said, "This piece was written about two hundred fifty years ago. What would you say about it?"

The answer came, "Cool, real cool. Lots better than the new stuff we're hearing, except for electronic rock, and that's so different you can't compare."

Hindemith's *Kleine Kammermusik* was next. The clarinetist asked, "Well, there's a nonelectric piece written only a few decades ago. What's your reaction to it?" Little hands shot up, and a child of six said confidently, "Pretty modern and very dull." A blonde with a pigtail said, "It's busy all right, but it's not all *right*." An étude by Elliott Carter was played. A fourth-grader said, "It's full of right wrong notes, if you know what I mean. It just doesn't make much sense . . . not to me it doesn't."

We'd better watch out. These tykes are hip.

Does Japan's industrial emergence have its parallel in musical art? Or, as Donal Henahan asked in his *New York Times* review of Teiko Maehashi's debut with the American Symphony, "Is there an underground factory in Japan manufacturing violin virtuosos?"

The answer is a hearty affirmitive, if we modify "violin virtuosos" to "excellent violinists, trained in the method of Shinichi Suzuki." Also the question should properly embrace other Oriental countries that have been producing not only string players but also conductors, pianists, and woodwind players, an astonishing number of whom have been creating excitement at Western concerts and contests during the last decade.

The list is already too long for inclusion here, but the Orientals are obviously producing musical performers in considerable quantity and of quality comparable to that of any other nation.

"You can't hinder the wind," wrote Carl Sandburg. This optimistic thought is being acted out in a college here, a university there, and in a few of the more alert conservatories. The astute music student and music lover may now find basic courses and extension courses, with and without college credits, in such timely studies as commercial instrumentation and arranging, composition techniques applied to advertising jingles, underscoring, and film music, from classical to rock. Also available are courses in the art of recording, the technology, repair, and maintenance of instruments, and, at long last, in the contemporary calligraphy of charts and designs, though they are still rare.

And for some time, such studies must necessarily be either scarce or ineffectual not only because our academic institutions are weighted down by so many economic vicissitudes, but also because, despite the best will in the world, our music schools are faced with a serious paucity of authoritative teachers who can be found let alone persuaded to teach, especially if engaged in the far more reward-ing commercial fields. Meanwhile time itself will again have to serve as the most available teacher.

In a last-minute survey, I traveled to several of our more restless college campuses, where I ques-tioned some two hundred music students and heard about one hundred of them in graduate recitals, contests, and informal performances. I found but fifteen whom I considered really talented and whose gifts had been professionally developed.

Why so few? Have standards of higher education so declined that degrees will soon be merely scraps of paper? Are we so stiffly democratic that we can't deny anyone a college education? Or are we finally being pushed to admit that, at this moment of our evolution, and in so specialized a field as musical performance, democracy just won't work? Perhaps there are not that many gifted people, and if there were, there are certainly not enough teachers equipped to guide their careers properly. Students today are very practical. They know when and also why they are not getting what they came for, and their revolutions, hard and soft, are essentially attempts to close the gap between academic life and life itself.

An unprecedented windfall descended benignly upon the New York State Council on the Arts when the state legislature voted a 1970–71 appropriation of over $18 million, more than our federal government had ever spent on the arts. Everyone was stunned, not excluding the legislators themselves, by the allocation of such a whopping sum to aid individual artists and organizations.

The council's executive director at the time, John Hightower, stated that special consideration would be given to requests that could be matched by funds from new sources and to those "that try to extend their cultural services and that can demonstrate need, cultural excellence, and administrative and managerial competence."

A down-to-earth statement. There is indeed an appalling shortage of people specifically qualified for the immensely important work of directing, managing, and administering the institutions of the arts. This has resulted in a considerable amount of justified criticism and in the withholding of broad financial support, especially by Big Business. A massive academic program should be instituted to attract and to develop administrative and managerial talents.

The need today of musical institutions for specialized executive experience was underlined by the New York Philharmonic Society's election of Carlos Mosley as its president and its appointment of Helen T. Thompson as its manager.

Mr. Mosley has impressive credentials, including graduation magna cum laude from Duke University, postgraduate work as a piano student of Olga Samaroff Stokowski, and directorship of the School of Music at the University of Oklahoma. These achievements—and many more—make Mosley not only the first full-time professional president of the Philharmonic Society but also the first professional musician in history to assume that position.

Helen Thompson is also one of a kind—the only woman to hold the managerial post of a current major American orchestra. And she has the further distinctions of a solid academic and instrumental background, besides almost three decades as executive vice-president and treasurer of the American Symphony Orchestra League.

When I asked her opinion of the hue and cry throughout the country to combat ever rising orchestral costs by combining several symphony groups of smaller communities, I was not aware that in the early forties Mrs. Thompson had managed the Charleston (West Virginia) Symphony, and I was therefore unprepared for her reply.

"We must not lose sight of the fact," she said, "that smaller orchestral efforts have been a tremendously significant factor in building new audiences for music everywhere. I'm convinced that the original allegiance to the hometown orchestra because it is 'ours' and 'local' slowly transfers itself to orchestras and orchestral music generally. Eventually, with a percentage of this new audience, musical taste and judgment, perception, and awareness of artistic excellence develop—and so, the cause of music *is* served. Smaller towns can do this in a way that metropolitan centers can't and they are doing it in communities all over this land."

The value of regionalism, on a scale never before attempted by a major symphony orchestra, is evidenced by the newly named Minnesota Orchestra, according to its forceful general manager, Richard M. Cisek. The objective of the former Minneapolis Symphony is to become a fifty-two week organization that serves not only the Twin

Cities but all of Minnesota rather than "a gypsy band trying to stay alive by cross-country tours" that are no longer profitable.

With its personnel's permission, the orchestra can be subdivided into smaller groups, a flexibility essential to the regional concept. In a venturesome experiment, the orchestra is being structured so as to facilitate advantageous university association, to become adaptable to children's programs, to operatic, theatrical, and dance groups, and to pops programs. "This orchestra also has to relate to other art organizations and must help them develop," Mr. Cisek said.

This bold, all-embracing plan has inspired the friendly rivalry of a rising young neighbor, the St. Paul Chamber Orchestra, whose slogan "Music on the Move," indicates its own regional goals. Facilitated by a unique union contract that permits absolute freedom in regrouping the basic twenty-two-man personnel into any "combo" desired, the members can function in any number of ways and places.

Stephen Sell, the group's visionary young manager, won national plaudits when he said, "People are becoming more and more reluctant to come to the center city for anything. If they are ever going to relate to small communities and suburbs, let's bring the music out to them. In our orchestra, we have a lot of swinging people and they aren't afraid to step out on their own."

The desperate need for a reorientation to the temper of audiences young and old, naive and sophisticated, urban and suburban, is also being articulated and activated in Los Angeles. Ernest Fleischmann is not only managing that city's orchestra but also demonstrating a far-ranging inventiveness and influence which are affecting that area's entire cultural climate.

Fleischmann has taken to the air to sell music, every sort of music, to one and all. He has expanded youth concerts in a formidable project which includes performances, demonstrations, and discussions in and out of classrooms, and which utilizes recordings, visual aids, and resource material. He has turned his powers of persuasion on parents, school teachers, and officials to encourage the youngsters by precept rather than preachment to "dig" music.

In concert halls, from Los Angeles to New York, on university campuses, on TV, and wherever else it has appeared, the versatile orchestra under the baton of Zubin Mehta has offered the "works," from jam sessions to peace demonstrations set to Handel's *Messiah*.

Fleischmann has said, "Any of my colleagues, I

am sure, can report similar exciting projects. . . . It is typical of what is happening on the American orchestral scene."

One could only wish that the comment were accurate but it isn't, except for a few centers such as St. Louis and Cleveland. Venturesome ideas and action are anything but typical. The facts indicate that the declining patronage of concerts and the disastrously descending market for recordings and publications of classical music are not only the result of inflation and the consequent cutback in purchasing power. A goodly portion of the distressing situation is due to insularity, lack of vision, and the scarcity of leadership such as I have described.

Another heartening exception is Julius Bloom, the ebullient executive director of the Carnegie Hall Corporation. While the heads of art institutions from coast to coast were grappling with a plunging economy, Mr. Bloom announced for 1970–71 a beneficent season of fifteen series of concerts to be presented at the celebrated hall, which supplement the many other events for which the hall is rented by outside auspices. "The sixty-eight events included in our series," says Bloom, cheerfully, "are only the forerunners of still other concerts (from solos to orchestras) to be sponsored by our corporation in what will unquestionably be the

210

busiest and most important season ever scheduled here."

Unquestionably, sir? Thanks for the optimism, and especially for the three series of six concerts each at Carnegie's annual International Festival of Visiting Orchestras, one of the most generous musical feasts obtainable anywhere here or abroad.

On the other hand, the Hunter College Concert Bureau, which is widely regarded as New York's most significant source of low-priced, non-orchestral concerts, is in serious jeopardy. An SOS was flashed in the form of an appeal for money from the bureau, which has neither needed nor received much subsidy from the college it serves so admirably, and has never before had to seek aid from its regular patrons.

The success and administrative record of this nonprofit organization are enviable. First administered by Norman Singer, now directing New York's City Center, it is presently headed by Omus Hirshbein, whose artistic and business acumen, personal force, and tact equip him ideally to direct this formidable entertainment project.

When I asked him for a statement, he said: "There's no use avoiding the facts: everyone in the arts is in unprecedented trouble today—ranging

211

from the need to curtail to the necessity to close
up. But many of our difficulties lie within our profession. For example, the whole concert picture
would improve instantly if the fees of individuals
and groups would be more flexibly scaled—suited
to the sheer ability of us buyers to pay, adjusted to
our specific setup—a policy that could be facilitated by more efficiently planned artists' itineraries.
Then, more imagination in the organization of
series so as to offer both variety and unity; the
same with individual programs. I assure you, the
box office instantly reflects the degree to which
performers show a realistic understanding of current audiences' need for a rich, varied, and vibrant
experience.

"One could go on and on, but merely discarding
damaging policies and actions would help save
many a musical ship that is listing badly or sink-
ing."

An unexpected meeting with Thomas Schippers
led to an informal chat with that eminent conductor, one of the tidiest thinkers in our profession. I
asked him if he could sum up "in a word" what
he has observed about the classical field and where
he thinks we're headed. He said, "I certainly
wouldn't risk any generalization or predictions. All
I know, really, is what everyone knows—that our

so-called and perhaps miscalled 'serious music' is in trouble.

"So many trends are moving in so many conflicting directions that they can't help overlapping. Audiences are obviously diminishing and costs are rising almost prohibitively, considering the insufficiency of subsidies in proportion to the needs. Yet, a vast amount of musical activity goes on willy-nilly, both performing, and composing. It ranges from terrible to terrific.

"Apropos, maybe the musical recession may not be an unmixed curse. I think that at long last the musician who can't or won't communicate today is beginning to see that he will not survive very much longer. Until around 1969, protective institutions and a permissive society allowed composers to avoid the basic responsibility—to communicate or to suffer the consequences. The public got what it permitted and deserved, and took it. Now that's about finished, thank goodness."

Schippers was stating a truism that Joseph Addison articulated over two hundred fifty years ago: that the quality of a society's art depends less on its artists than upon what it demands from its artists.

In the midst of the musical recession, there is one exception so astonishing that it could serve to

213

break rather than to prove any of the current "rules" of the concert world.

In 1968, when the orchestras of every city were already in real trouble, Newark, New Jersey, was bitten by the symphony bug. The conductorial post was offered to Henry Lewis, who thereupon became the first black to direct a metropolitan orchestra in the United States. He took over a pick-up group of "avocational musicians," which played a season of twenty-two concerts on a $75,-000 budget.

Today, a splendidly trained major orchestra of eighty-seven professionals plus "some ardent amateurs" plays one hundred concerts a year in eight cities on a budget of $850,000. Solid support comes from Jersey communities that pack virtually every concert, and from federal, state, and municipal subsidies. The Mellon and Ford foundations have given handsome sums and have inspired private contributions. The orchestral board has five blacks on it; the Newark series has a black doctor as its honorary president. When Lewis took over, there was one black player. Now there are eight.

"Pupils from the schools are bussed in for fifty youth concerts we're giving this year," said Mr. Lewis. "We also do one dollar regular concerts in Newark, a series of three family programs that have been drawing capacity audiences of twenty-five hundred people—50 to 75 per cent of them black. You see," he added, "Newark is more than 60 per cent black and Puerto Rican and the focus must change to include their interests."

Mr. Lewis must be doing *everything* right. His orchestra is admirable, his programs distinguished. He makes no "compromises," no show of exhibitionism, none of temperament except in the music itself, where he is implicitly obeyed. Everything about his concerts, orchestra, programs, audiences, himself, is completely representative of the community life, whether the events are being staged in a big auditorium or outdoors in the ghetto neighborhoods.

"We've proved that we can succeed," he said. "We are wanted by our audiences. Our project is a symbol. It means that all is not lost, and that symphonic music is still relevant."

Two authoritative and revealing surveys were issued in 1970, one by the oldest of the nonprofit managements, the National Music League, and the other by the Association of College and University Concert Managers. Following are some brief summaries that delineate data pertinent to our inquiries.

The NML report, analyzed by Dwight Cooke, states that "an important reason for the decrease in the young artist's solo appearance opportunities is the noticeable reduction in the growth rate of live audiences . . . concert audiences are not increasing in proportion to the population increase . . . and in particular, concerts are not attracting the younger, under-twenty-five-year-olds needed for healthy audience replenishment." This in turn is seen "as a direct reflection of the decline in music education in the home and in schools."

In summary, the survey concludes that "there is a future for live serious music and for the young solo musician, but it is along a narrowing path. Respondents show a deep desire to widen that path, but they need help to do it." And how! The blunt cool of the statistical surveys is that only about 2 per cent of Americans go to musical events, including those that offer free admission.

The ACUCM report, analyzed and tabulated by Robert Moon and Norman Kaderlan, both of the University of Wisconsin, discloses that attendance at 36 per cent of all its respondents' events "was less than 60 per cent of capacity; 19 per cent of all concerts were sold out (rock, ballet, symphony, in that order, register highest gross attendance over-all); 7 per cent of all concerts had attendance less than 20 per cent of capacity; attendance at 40 per cent of all events drew over 80 per cent of capacity."

216

In summary, the survey shows that rock events do best, symphony concerts relatively well (71 per cent of capacity) and vocal recitals, instrumental recitals, and chamber music do worst, in that order. It also states that "three out of four of the highest student-attended *classical art forms* have *visual components*."

In 1971, a new national organization, Partnership of the Arts, was formed under the direction of Amyas Ames, chairman of Lincoln Center. The aim of this coordinated voluntary group of cultural institutions "is to call public attention to the na-

GOVERNMENT SUPPORT OF THE ARTS IN 1970

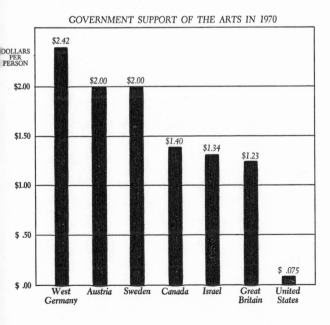

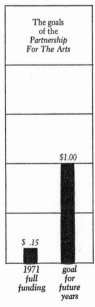

tionwide plight of the arts," a plight dramatically illustrated by comparative graphs as self-explanatory as they are deplorable.

Another graph denotes a goal of $200 million federal funding annually, which Mr. Ames said would represent $1 per person in the United States . . . and only 1 per cent of what we now spend on our highways."

The Kennedy Center of the Performing Arts, after a decade of vacillation and stagnation, is finally a reality. The vast Washington compound houses four theaters, an imposing 2,700-seat concert hall, a 2,200-seat opera house, a 1,100-seat drama building, and a 500-seat cinema.

This is the architectural layout. As to the artistic planning, one hopes that the dedicatory events offered no prospectus of the future.

Leonard Bernstein's *Mass,* Alberto Ginastera's opera *Beatrix Cenci,* and an orchestral program provided opportunities to hear Washington's major musical organizations. They also provided opportunities to observe to what extent the props of sanctity are being substituted for religious faith, melodrama for creative power, and exterior glamour for excellence. The *Mass* is an eclectic and simplistic attempt to express humanity's gravest crises; the opera is still another version of two earlier

218

Ginastera operas, with extra pinches of incestuous rape and murder; and our capital's orchestra has yet to become a major symphonic organization.

The viability of this new cultural center will depend upon the degree to which it reflects not only the highest national goals but also the community's artistic and intellectual needs. The meek shall *not* inherit another marble mausoleum. Nor will standardization work much longer, as indicated by the reactions to the "sure-fire" program, which began with Beethoven's *Consecration of the House* Overture. It is no longer sure-fire because it is no longer interesting to the "mass audience"—a term that no longer carries its former connotations. If anyone doubts that, I recommend a careful study of the ACUCM's survey that I mentioned.

On every campus, just as there is growing distrust and disdain of routine curricula, so there is increasing disapproval of those who have been booking and managing cultural events.

The young people have begun to take matters into their own hands. Early in 1970, the students of a state university in Ohio decided to hold a creative arts festival. Their elected representatives engaged a group of some of our most provocative artists from the fields of sculpture, painting, poetry, drama, and music. With admirable economic fi-

219

nesse, the youngsters presented them in a week of imaginative and stimulating activities on a budget of $12,000—less than a third of what it had cost a month before to bring Johnny Carson's show to the campus for one night.

It was heartening to witness the triumph of the festival, to see that at least in some places fresh air is let in so that the arts can breathe and expand. But how many people had then even heard of Kent State? Like many of our country's rapidly maturing state universities, Kent was flourishing in an obscurity out of all connection with its intellectual, spiritual, and artistic vigor.

Then a volley of gunfire heard round the world brought a tragic fame to this campus, on which four of its promising members lay slain. Our nation has been fundamentally affected. Perhaps it is not unrealistic to hope that the students' role in America's political awakening may be replayed in America's artistic awakening.

In Los Angeles, I tackled a musical "man for all seasons," one of those free-lance performers who can play anything anywhere at the astronomical pay scale of nonclassical dates. A former first clarinetist of a great East Coast orchestra, and one of the most intelligent and articulate musicians I encountered in my fact-finding forays, he said: "You want to know what caused me to leave the first chair of a great orchestra to play this jingle track? Sit down, it'll take more than a minute. Just keep me nameless, please.

"First, let's start with the bread-and-butter department. Every time the damned contract came up, there was another crisis—could we go on or would we fold? We felt like beggars, hats in hand, and for what? Peanuts, even if we got what we asked for—much less than a truck driver gets, and nothing compared to a plumber.

"Now, from the musical angle. Actually, it's almost as important because the financial sacrifice I always expected to make. But finally, it was the concerts themselves, all the pretentious crap that got me down. No matter what the critics said, no matter how the public reacted, the same stupid policies that have damned-near killed music ever since the twelve-tone epidemic started—and that's almost seventy years ago—still went on and are still going on right now. I think the classical musicians are the dumbest, the most suicidal bastards who ever lived.

"Especially those egomaniacal conductors! They want to prove their 'open-mindedness' about modern music, and all they do is expose their ignorance, historical more than musical even. They're scared to death of the academic eunuchs, they're

221

scared maybe they'll lose a possible place in history if they turn down something nobody can understand—that's the extent of their insecurity.

"They don't know as much as their orchestra players, believe me. They're still trying to impress God-knows-who-or-why by programing stuff so confusing, so screwy, that we can't play it. The audience grins and bears it. Then comes the baloney: 'It is our *duty* to play it, so that the public can hear it.' Most of 'em don't even know that they're talking nonsense, that the public *has* listened and listened until it's had an earful and a bellyful, and that this has had a lot to do with what's wrong with the concert business.

"The orchestra men hate the stuff as much as the audience. But we were almost as bored by the standard stuff, especially by the newest 'reading' of some pet war horse by the current glamour boy to woo the audience back from the contemporary bunk, and wow 'em. It became a farce. Finally, I had it up to my bald spot and I quit."

I asked him if he thought that the concert business was on its way out. "No, I don't think so. It's still breathing, and there'll always be an audience for the mainstays of the classical repertory. But I think the serial stuff is played out except in those vacuums called college music departments. If not for those 'nurseries,' the atonal boys would starve to death. They're dying anyway, and a few of 'em know it, but the trouble is the schools don't know what to *do* about it. I do. Their teachers need teachers."

I met another former first-desk player of a major symphony, also working in and around Hollywood. He is a fine violinist who started to become a soloist, broke his heart and pocketbook and health over it, became concertmaster of the second-fiddle section of an East Coast symphony, threw in the towel, and went West. He is now in tremendous demand for commercial work, but also teaches violin at a California university. His answers to my general inquiries merit complete quotation.

"Do you know," he said, "if not for my commercial experience, I'd feel like a whore teaching youngsters with professional hopes today. Don't ask me where music's going or anything like that, but I know that violinists are going to have less and less chance to make a living in symphony orchestras because there'll be fewer and fewer. Not because this rich country can't subsidize them. Wars or no wars, we could do it right now. But we're not moving in that direction. Not the government, not the universities or cultural institutions or classical musicians or the music public.

"That much I know. What else I know is that the only excitement and vitality and real freshness

223

I've struck in over twenty years of knocking around the music world has been mainly in the pop field, and in every part of it—jazz, film scores, rock, folk-rhythm-and-blues, and so on. A lot of it is just terrible, just as awful as the classical serial junk, but at least more honest because so much of what's bad is plain ignorance.

"Anyway, here's what I'm telling my pupils: learn as much as you can about everything—about your main instrument, for example, and then learn another instrument, a useful one like a horn or a clarinet or drums; learn the new notation and how to improvise; learn other languages, get a smattering of physics, and learn to manipulate tape, recording machines, and synthesizers, because that's where music's going, to an electronic environment.

"Already, we're seeing new things coming up every day, and some of it is provocative and even promising. I guarantee you, *my* pupils will be able to handle it—any part of it."

All around us are the confusions and contradictions of a revolutionary age, in which every manifestation of the "new" seems still young, no matter how long it has been functioning.

In the classical field, Pierre Boulez recently introduced his latest composition, *Pli Selon Pli*, an hour-long orchestral work on which he had been laboring for almost twenty years. This large-scale piece of serial music seems as inaccessible and remote as the lost, sunken city that "inspired" it.

But Boulez, the conductor of the New York Philharmonic, is presenting four special concerts of what appears to be an advance unit of musical Utopia known now as The Free Music Store, whose "extravaganzas" in downtown New York featured the latest permutations of whatever represented "an honest effort to break new ground."

In the jazz field, Yusef Lateef has completed *Symphonic Blues Suite*, an ambitious twenty-five minute work for string quartet and orchestra. Utilizing many Eastern instruments and rich harmonizations, this versatile musician has created distinctive sonorities that are in themselves fascinating. Like Duke Ellington, however, the composer-flutist has so far failed in his larger works to achieve the dramatic development and that sense of momentum so essential to the realization of spacious art forms.

As for rock, it is hardly snuggled safely in any bed of roses. Signs of the times on an international scale arose during the Isle of Wight Festival, which drew 250,000 Britons, Americans, Frenchmen, Germans, Italians, Swedes, and Danes. Joan Baez, Jimi Hendrix, Donovan, Ritchie Havens, Tiny Tim, Miles Davis, and Joni Mitchell were among the star attractions in a pop fest that ended in violence, bitterness, and vandalism.

And quite recently, a so-called medieval rock opera, *The Survival of St. Joan,* made a disastrous debut. "The book is preposterous," reported Clive Barnes in the *Times,* also describing the other elements as "pretentious nonsense, that tries to be modern, modish, fashionable, and even significant . . . but has little to declare besides its quite remarkable impudence."

The rock movement suffered a body blow when Fillmore East and Fillmore West folded during the summer of 1971. Boss Bill Graham, who always enjoyed a reputation for having a prophetic sense of timing, had long maintained that "the concert racket, classical and pop, is just dryin' up." The clincher might well have been an appearance by the mighty James Taylor, who vainly tried to make contact with the customers, dozens of whom had dozed off locked in each other's arms, and who remained fast asleep even when a monstrously juiced-up sound system amplified Taylor's every whisper into a roar. Calling quits, Graham said, "The new music-goer ain't bringin' in no class with him. Dig it? He ain't bringin' in no class."

Remember when "country music" reflected its essential role as the emotionally charged art form

226

of the sultry, rural South? Now see what the revolution hath wrought!

Country music has become cool, conscious, populist, and thoroughly urbanized, like its audience. Social injustice, political skullduggery, cheats who buy "Cadilacs" on welfare money, are its subjects now. The sounds have a beat and a smell of another sort of "grass." Here and there, a touch of religion, a patriotic phrase, or a poetically moving modulation will recall the old South. But as for making a body muse nostalgically or whistle "Dixie," forget it. Just chalk up one more casualty of the times.

All of this is part of the growing-up process. Isn't it?

What I had hoped, perhaps naively, to make a systematic report or a tidy summation of the field of instrumental music winds up as neither. Perhaps in this ferment of unconstrained activities, complete consistency is as unattainable as completeness.

The reader may well ask, nevertheless, what I have asked myself time and again during my years of inquiry: does the forseeable future of classical music justify optimism? The best answer I can venture is a guarded yes and no, for the paradoxes

227

inherent in musical art are no less contradictory than those to be found in the world itself. Perhaps in art they appear more incongruous because in art alone has man, through supreme individuality, attained perfection. Yet if one common denominator emerges more frequently than another from our chaotic society, it is the individual's feeling of utter helplessness against inexorable and soulless forces that he can neither understand nor control.

We see it on all sides: baby-faced youngsters caught in the draft and ordered to murder defenseless women and children; ambitious men and women laid off work to join millions of other unemployed citizens; a nation that can no longer afford to be sick; and mayors, governors, and even a president hurling imprecations at each other and at corporations and unions they can no longer influence. No wonder the individual, no matter who he is, comes to the melancholy conviction of being hopelessly trapped.

And yet, and yet, great movements are afoot: in civil rights, in enfranchisement of the young, in ecology, even in government. Never has there been more individual and collective concern and awareness on the part of our people, or more motivation to question every policy and politician, to do the decent thing, to regain for our country its prestige and dignity, to scrutinize organizations, committees, budgets, priorities, and to decry prejudice, exploitation, and injustice.

There we have the paradox: paralysis and pollution marching side by side with unprecedented progress in spirit and in decisive action. Is anything rational in these irrational times? Is it rational, for example, that at this moment of economic stringency so severe that federal funds for education are shrinking daily, President Nixon has asked Congress to appropriate $60 million for the National Arts and Humanities endowments, $30 million for each?

It scarcely matters whether the Ninety-second Congress, confronted for the first time with our monstrous budget, will go along. The president's recommendation remains both an enigma and a milestone, along with his stated hope that the unprecedented sum will "provide consistent, substantial support in a partnership that avoids government domination and encourages institutional and artistic independence . . . and will so enable more young people to be brought into greater involvement with the arts and humanities."

Alongside federal subsidies to American farmers, to the oil industry, and to the airlines, the amount requested for the arts and humanities is a plea for pennies, of course. Yet, it appears to be a healthy recognition that the arts are not businesses ex-

229

pected to yield profits, that essentially they are national treasures that must be supported.

And it just may be an omen of a changing America.

Index

231

Chicago College of Music, 78

Chopin, Frédéric, 108, 140

Chopin Competition, 94, 101, 108

Cincinnati, University of, 63

Cisek, Richard M., 207–208

City Center, 211

Cleveland Institute, 78

Cleveland Symphony, 107

Cliburn, Van, 41, 91–92, 97, 98, 101, 103, 105, 108, 122, 126

Colbert, Ann, 115, 129

Coleman, Ornette, 171

Collins, Judy, 173

Columbia Artists Management, Inc., 81, 115

Columbia Broadcasting System, 172

Columbia-Princeton Electronic Music Center, 82, 186, 188

Columbia University, 63, 166

"Come Sunday," 197

Community Concerts, 115

Como, Perry, 95

competitions, 92–112; *see also* specific names

computer music, 187, 199

Concerned Musicians Association, 44–45

Concert Artists Guild, 125–126

Concert Club, 126–127

concert managers, 113–131; *see also* specific names

Concerto in B-flat Minor (Tchaikovsky), 109

Consecration of the House (Beethoven), 219

Cooke, Dwight, 215–216

Copland, Aaron, 3, 23

Cornell University, 62

country-and-western, 9, 12–14, 226–227

Couperin, François, 18

Cowell, Henry, 21

Crosby, Bing, 147

"Cultural Festival" (Mount Morris Park), 172

Curtis Institute of Music, 78

Cusumano, Roy, 59

Danziger, Harris, 25, 26, 27, 65

Davis, Miles, 225

Debussy, Claude, 3, 23, 192

Debut-Award Concerts, 125

Dichter, Misha, 98–99, 102, 124

di Lasso, Orlando, 25

Dispeker, Thea, 128–129

Donovan, 173, 225

Downes, Olin, 139

Dudley, Raymond, 63

Duke University, 206

Du Pré, Jacqueline, 95

Dylan, Bob, 88, 173, 176, 177, 195–197

Eastman School, 78

Economic Dilemma of the Performing Arts, 47

E-flat Concerto (Liszt), 59

Electric Circus, 16, 19, 20, 176

electronic music, 6–7, 17, 19–20, 24, 29, 48, 81, 82, 87, 90, 179–180, 185–193, 199–200, 202